YARN Essentials

A comprehensive, hands-on guide to install, administer, and configure settings in YARN

Amol Fasale

Nirmal Kumar

BIRMINGHAM - MUMBAI

YARN Essentials

First published: February 2015

Production reference: 1190215

Published by Packt Publishing Ltd.
Livery Place
35 Livery Street
Birmingham B3 2PB, UK.

ISBN 978-1-78439-173-7

www.packtpub.com

Credits

Authors
Amol Fasale
Nirmal Kumar

Reviewers
Lakshmi Narasimhan
Swapnil Salunkhe
Jenny (Xiao) Zhang

Commissioning Editor
Taron Pereira

Acquisition Editor
James Jones

Content Development Editor
Arwa Manasawala

Technical Editor
Indrajit A. Das

Copy Editors
Karuna Narayanan
Laxmi Subramanian

Project Coordinator
Purav Motiwalla

Proofreaders
Safis Editing
Maria Gould

Indexer
Priya Sane

Graphics
Sheetal Aute
Valentina D'silva
Abhinash Sahu

Production Coordinator
Shantanu N. Zagade

Cover Work
Shantanu N. Zagade

About the Authors

Amol Fasale has more than 4 years of industry experience actively working in the fields of big data and distributed computing; he is also an active blogger in and contributor to the open source community. Amol works as a senior data system engineer at MakeMyTrip.com, a very well-known travel and hospitality portal in India, responsible for real-time personalization of online user experience with Apache Kafka, Apache Storm, Apache Hadoop, and many more. Also, Amol has active hands-on experience in Java/J2EE, Spring Frameworks, Python, machine learning, Hadoop framework components, SQL, NoSQL, and graph databases.

You can follow Amol on Twitter at `@amolfasale` or on LinkedIn. Amol is very active on social media. You can catch him online for any technical assistance; he would be happy to help.

Amol has completed his bachelor's in engineering (electronics and telecommunication) from Pune University and postgraduate diploma in computers from CDAC.

The gift of love is one of the greatest blessings from parents, and I am heartily thankful to my mom, dad, friends, and colleagues who have shown and continue to show their support in different ways. Finally, I owe much to James and Arwa without whose direction and understanding, I would not have completed this work.

Nirmal Kumar is a lead software engineer at iLabs, the R&D team at Impetus Infotech Pvt. Ltd. He has more than 8 years of experience in open source technologies such as Java, JEE, Spring, Hibernate, web services, Hadoop, Hive, Flume, Sqoop, Kafka, Storm, NoSQL databases such as HBase and Cassandra, and MPP databases such as Teradata.

You can follow him on Twitter at `@nirmal___kumar`. He spends most of his time reading about and playing with different technologies. He has also undertaken many tech talks and training sessions on big data technologies.

He has attained his master's degree in computer applications from Harcourt Butler Technological Institute (HBTI), Kanpur, India and is currently part of the big data R&D team in iLabs at Impetus Infotech Pvt. Ltd.

I would like to thank my organization, especially iLabs, for supporting me in writing this book. Also, a special thanks to the Packt Publishing team; without you guys, this work would not have been possible.

About the Reviewers

Lakshmi Narasimhan is a full stack developer who has been working on big data and search since the early days of Lucene and was a part of the search team at Ask.com. He is a big advocate of open source and regularly contributes and consults on various technologies, most notably Drupal and technologies related to big data. Lakshmi is currently working as the curriculum designer for his own training company, `http://www.readybrains.com`. He blogs occasionally about his technical endeavors at `http://www.lakshminp.com` and can be contacted via his Twitter handle, `@lakshminp`.

It's hard find a ready reference or documentation for a subject like YARN. I'd like to thank the author for writing a book on YARN and hope the target audience finds it useful.

Swapnil Salunkhe is a passionate software developer who is keenly interested in learning and implementing new technologies. He has a passion for functional programming, machine learning, and working with data. He has experience working in the finance and telecom domains.

I'd like to thank Packt Publishing and its staff for an opportunity to contribute to this book.

Jenny (Xiao) Zhang is a technology professional in business analytics, KPIs, and big data. She helps businesses better manage, measure, report, and analyze data to answer critical business questions and drive business growth. She is an expert in SaaS business and had experience in a variety of industry domains such as telecom, oil and gas, and finance. She has written a number of blog posts at `http://jennyxiaozhang.com` on big data, Hadoop, and YARN. She also actively uses Twitter at `@smallnaruto` to share insights on big data and analytics.

I want to thank all my blog readers. It is the encouragement from them that motivates me to deep dive into the ocean of big data. I also want to thank my dad, Michael (Tiegang) Zhang, for providing technical insights in the process of reviewing the book. A special thanks to the Packt Publishing team for this great opportunity.

www.PacktPub.com

Support files, eBooks, discount offers, and more

For support files and downloads related to your book, please visit `www.PacktPub.com`.

Did you know that Packt offers eBook versions of every book published, with PDF and ePub files available? You can upgrade to the eBook version at `www.PacktPub.com` and as a print book customer, you are entitled to a discount on the eBook copy. Get in touch with us at `service@packtpub.com` for more details.

At `www.PacktPub.com`, you can also read a collection of free technical articles, sign up for a range of free newsletters and receive exclusive discounts and offers on Packt books and eBooks.

`https://www2.packtpub.com/books/subscription/packtlib`

Do you need instant solutions to your IT questions? PacktLib is Packt's online digital book library. Here, you can search, access, and read Packt's entire library of books.

Why subscribe?

- Fully searchable across every book published by Packt
- Copy and paste, print, and bookmark content
- On demand and accessible via a web browser

Free access for Packt account holders

If you have an account with Packt at `www.PacktPub.com`, you can use this to access PacktLib today and view 9 entirely free books. Simply use your login credentials for immediate access.

Table of Contents

Preface

In a short span of time, YARN has attained a great deal of momentum and acceptance in the big data world.

YARN essentials is about YARN—the modern operating system for Hadoop. This book contains all that you need to know about YARN, right from its inception to the present and future.

In the first part of the book, you will be introduced to the motivation behind the development of YARN and learn about its core architecture, installation, and administration. This part also talks about the architectural differences that YARN brings to Hadoop 2 with respect to Hadoop 1 and why this redesign was needed.

In the second part, you will learn how to write a YARN application, how to submit an application to YARN, and how to monitor the application. Next, you will learn about the various emerging open source frameworks that are developed to run on top of YARN. You will learn to develop and deploy some use case examples using Apache Samza and Storm YARN.

Finally, we will talk about the failures in YARN, some alternative solutions available on the market, and the future and support for YARN in the big data world.

What this book covers

Chapter 1, Need for YARN, discusses the motivation behind the development of YARN. This chapter discusses what YARN is and why it is needed.

Chapter 2, YARN Architecture, is a deep dive into YARN's architecture. All the major components and their inner workings are explained in this chapter.

Chapter 3, YARN Installation, describes the steps required to set up a single-node and fully-distributed YARN cluster. It also talks about the important configurations/ properties that you should be aware of while installing the YARN cluster.

Chapter 4, YARN and Hadoop Ecosystems, talks about Hadoop with respect to YARN. It gives a short introduction to the Hadoop 1.x version, the architectural differences between Hadoop 1.x and Hadoop 2.x, and where exactly YARN fits into Hadoop 2.x.

Chapter 5, YARN Administration, covers information on the administration of YARN clusters. It explains the administrative tools that are available in YARN, what they mean, and how to use them. This chapter covers various topics from YARN container allocation and configuration to various scheduling policies/configurations and in-built support for multitenancy.

Chapter 6, Developing and Running a Simple YARN Application, focuses on some real applications with YARN, with some hands-on examples. It explains how to write a YARN application, how to submit an application to YARN, and finally, how to monitor the application.

Chapter 7, YARN Frameworks, discusses the various emerging open source frameworks that are developed to run on top of YARN. The chapter then talks in detail about Apache Samza and Storm on YARN, where we will develop and run some sample applications using these frameworks.

Chapter 8, Failures in YARN, discusses the fault-tolerance aspect of YARN. This chapter focuses on various failures that can occur in the YARN framework, their causes, and how YARN gracefully handles those failures.

Chapter 9, YARN – Alternative Solutions, discusses other alternative solutions that are available on the market today. These systems, like YARN, share common inspiration/ requirements and the high-level goal of improving scalability, latency, fault-tolerance, and programming model flexibility. This chapter highlights the key differences in the way these alternative solutions address the same features provided by YARN.

Chapter 10, YARN Future and Support, talks about YARN's journey and its present and future in the world of distributed computing.

What you need for this book

You will need a single Linux-based machine with JDK 1.6 or later installed. Any recent version of the Apache Hadoop 2 distribution will be sufficient to set up a YARN cluster and run some examples on top of YARN.

The code in this book has been tested on CentOS 6.4 but will run on other variants of Linux.

Who this book is for

This book is for the big data enthusiasts who want to gain in-depth knowledge of YARN and know what really makes YARN the modern operating system for Hadoop. You will develop a good understanding of the architectural differences that YARN brings to Hadoop 2 with respect to Hadoop 1.

You will develop in-depth knowledge about the architecture and inner workings of the YARN framework.

After finishing this book, you will be able to install, administrate, and develop YARN applications. This book tells you anything you need to know about YARN, right from its inception to its present and future in the big data industry.

Conventions

In this book, you will find a number of text styles that distinguish between different kinds of information. Here are some examples of these styles and an explanation of their meaning.

Code words in text, database table names, folder names, filenames, file extensions, pathnames, dummy URLs, user input, and Twitter handles are shown as follows: " The URL for NameNode is `http://<namenode_host>:<port>/` and the default HTTP port is `50070`."

A block of code is set as follows:

```
<property>
 <name>io.file.buffer.size</name>
 <value>4096</value>
 <description>read and write buffer size of files</description>
</property>
```

Any command-line input or output is written as follows:

```
${path_to_your_input_dir}
${path_to_your_output_dir_old}
```

New terms and **important words** are shown in bold. Words that you see on the screen, for example, in menus or dialog boxes, appear in the text like this: "Under the **Tools** section, you can find the YARN configuration file details, scheduling information, container configurations, local logs of the jobs, and a lot of other information on the cluster."

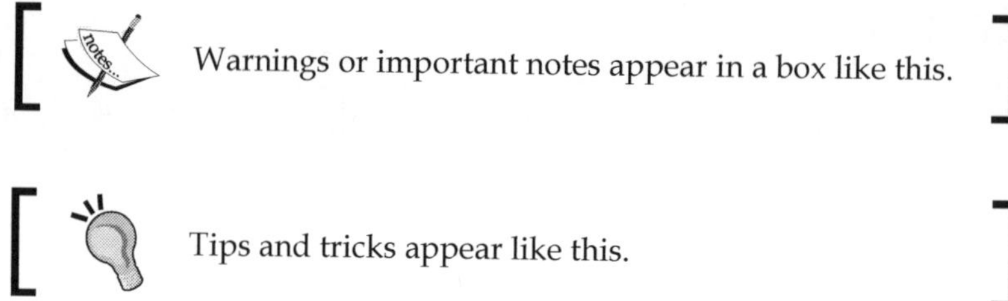

Warnings or important notes appear in a box like this.

Tips and tricks appear like this.

Reader feedback

Feedback from our readers is always welcome. Let us know what you think about this book—what you liked or disliked. Reader feedback is important for us as it helps us develop titles that you will really get the most out of.

To send us general feedback, simply e-mail `feedback@packtpub.com`, and mention the book's title in the subject of your message.

If there is a topic that you have expertise in and you are interested in either writing or contributing to a book, see our author guide at `www.packtpub.com/authors`.

Customer support

Now that you are the proud owner of a Packt book, we have a number of things to help you to get the most from your purchase.

Downloading the example code

You can download the example code files from your account at `http://www.packtpub.com` for all the Packt Publishing books you have purchased. If you purchased this book elsewhere, you can visit `http://www.packtpub.com/support` and register to have the files e-mailed directly to you.

Errata

Although we have taken every care to ensure the accuracy of our content, mistakes do happen. If you find a mistake in one of our books—maybe a mistake in the text or the code—we would be grateful if you could report this to us. By doing so, you can save other readers from frustration and help us improve subsequent versions of this book. If you find any errata, please report them by visiting `http://www.packtpub.com/submit-errata`, selecting your book, clicking on the **Errata Submission Form** link, and entering the details of your errata. Once your errata are verified, your submission will be accepted and the errata will be uploaded to our website or added to any list of existing errata under the Errata section of that title.

To view the previously submitted errata, go to `https://www.packtpub.com/books/content/support` and enter the name of the book in the search field. The required information will appear under the **Errata** section.

Piracy

Piracy of copyrighted material on the Internet is an ongoing problem across all media. At Packt, we take the protection of our copyright and licenses very seriously. If you come across any illegal copies of our works in any form on the Internet, please provide us with the location address or website name immediately so that we can pursue a remedy.

Please contact us at `copyright@packtpub.com` with a link to the suspected pirated material.

We appreciate your help in protecting our authors and our ability to bring you valuable content.

Questions

If you have a problem with any aspect of this book, you can contact us at `questions@packtpub.com`, and we will do our best to address the problem.

1
Need for YARN

YARN stands for **Yet Another Resource Negotiator**. YARN is a generic resource platform to manage resources in a typical cluster. YARN was introduced with Hadoop 2.0, which is an open source distributed processing framework from the Apache Software Foundation.

In 2012, YARN became one of the subprojects of the larger Apache Hadoop project. YARN is also coined by the name of MapReduce 2.0. This is since Apache Hadoop MapReduce has been re-architectured from the ground up to Apache Hadoop YARN.

Think of YARN as a generic computing fabric to support MapReduce and other application paradigms within the same Hadoop cluster; earlier, this was limited to batch processing using MapReduce. This really changed the game to recast Apache Hadoop as a much more powerful data processing system. With the advent of YARN, Hadoop now looks very different compared to the way it was only a year ago.

YARN enables multiple applications to run simultaneously on the same shared cluster and allows applications to negotiate resources based on need. Therefore, resource allocation/management is central to YARN.

YARN has been thoroughly tested at Yahoo! since September 2012. It has been in production across 30,000 nodes and 325 PB of data since January 2013.

Recently, Apache Hadoop YARN won the *Best Paper Award* at ACM **Symposium on Cloud Computing** (**SoCC**) in 2013!

The redesign idea

Initially, Hadoop was written solely as a MapReduce engine. Since it runs on a cluster, its cluster management components were also tightly coupled with the MapReduce programming paradigm.

The concepts of MapReduce and its programming paradigm were so deeply ingrained in Hadoop that one could not use it for anything else except MapReduce. MapReduce therefore became the base for Hadoop, and as a result, the only thing that could be run on Hadoop was a MapReduce job, batch processing. In Hadoop 1.x, there was a single JobTracker service that was overloaded with many things such as cluster resource management, scheduling jobs, managing computational resources, restarting failed tasks, monitoring TaskTrackers, and so on.

There was definitely a need to separate the MapReduce (specific programming model) part and the resource management infrastructure in Hadoop. YARN was the first attempt to perform this separation.

Limitations of the classical MapReduce or Hadoop 1.x

The main limitations of Hadoop 1.x can be categorized into the following areas:

- Limited scalability:
    - Large Hadoop clusters reported some serious limitations on scalability. This is caused mainly by a single JobTracker service, which ultimately results in a serious deterioration of the overall cluster performance because of attempts to re-replicate data and overload live nodes, thus causing a network flood.
    - According to Yahoo!, the practical limits of such a design are reached with a cluster of ~5,000 nodes and 40,000 tasks running concurrently. Therefore, it is recommended that you create smaller and less powerful clusters for such a design.
- Low cluster resource utilization:
    - The resources in Hadoop 1.x on each slave node (data node), are divided in terms of a fixed number of map and reduce slots.
    - Consider the scenario where a MapReduce job has already taken up all the available map slots and now wants more new map tasks to run. In this case, it cannot run new map tasks, even though all the reduce slots are still empty. This notion of a fixed number of slots has a serious drawback and results in poor cluster utilization.

- Lack of support for alternative frameworks/paradigms:
    - The main focus of Hadoop right from the beginning was to perform computation on large datasets using parallel processing.
    - Therefore, the only programming model it supported was MapReduce.
    - With the current industry needs in terms of new use cases in the world of big data, many new and alternative programming models (such Apache Giraph, Apache Spark, Storm, Tez, and so on) are coming into the picture each day. There is definitely an increasing demand to support multiple programming paradigms besides MapReduce, to support the varied use cases that the big data world is facing.

YARN as the modern operating system of Hadoop

The MapReduce programming model is, no doubt, great for many applications, but not for everything in the world of computation. There are use cases that are best suited for MapReduce, but not all.

MapReduce is essentially batch-oriented, but support for real-time and near real-time processing are the emerging requirements in the field of big data.

YARN took cluster resource management capabilities from the MapReduce system so that new engines could use these generic cluster resource management capabilities. This lightened up the MapReduce system to focus on the data processing part, which it is good at and will ideally continue to be so.

YARN therefore turns into a data operating system for Hadoop 2.0, as it enables multiple applications to coexist in the same shared cluster. Refer to the following figure:

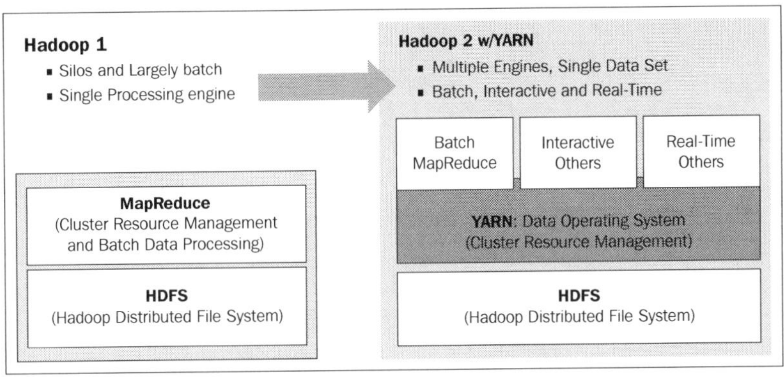

YARN as a modern OS for Hadoop

at are the design goals for YARN

ection talks about the core design goals of YARN:

- Scalability:
    - Scalability is a key requirement for big data. Hadoop was primarily meant to work on a cluster of thousands of nodes with commodity hardware. Also, the cost of hardware is reducing year-on-year.
    - YARN is therefore designed to perform efficiently on this network of a myriad of nodes.
- High cluster utilization:
    - In Hadoop 1.x, the cluster resources were divided in terms of fixed size slots for both map and reduce tasks. This means that there could be a scenario where map slots might be full while reduce slots are empty, or vice versa. This was definitely not an optimal utilization of resources, and it needed further optimization.
    - YARN fine-grained resources in terms of RAM, CPU, and disk (containers), leading to an optimal utilization of the available resources.
- Locality awareness:
    - This is a key requirement for YARN when dealing with big data; moving computation is cheaper than moving data.
    - This helps to minimize network congestion and increase the overall throughput of the system.
- Multitenancy:
    - With the core development of Hadoop at Yahoo, primarily to support large-scale computation, HDFS also acquired a permission model, quotas, and other features to improve its multitenant operation.
    - YARN was therefore designed to support multitenancy in its core architecture. Since cluster resource allocation/management is at the heart of YARN, sharing processing and storage capacity across clusters was central to the design.
    - YARN has the notion of pluggable schedulers and the Capacity Scheduler with YARN has been enhanced to provide a flexible resource model, elastic computing, application limits, and other necessary features that enable multiple tenants to securely share the cluster in an optimized way.

- Support for programming model:
    - The MapReduce programming model is no doubt great for many applications, but not for everything in the world of computation.
    - As the world of big data is still in its inception phase, organizations are heavily investing in R&D to develop new and evolving frameworks to solve a variety of problems that big data brings.
- A flexible resource model:
    - Besides mismatch with the emerging frameworks' requirements, the fixed number of slots for resources had serious problems. It was straightforward for YARN to come up with a flexible and generic resource management model.
- A secure and auditable operation:
    - As Hadoop continued to grow to manage more tenants with a myriad of use cases across different industries, the requirements for isolation became more demanding.
    - Also, the authorization model lacked strong and scalable authentication. This is because Hadoop was designed with parallel processing in mind, with no comprehensive security. Security was an afterthought.
    - YARN understands this and adds security-related requirements into its design.
- Reliability/availability:
    - Although fault tolerance is in the core design, in reality maintaining a large Hadoop cluster is a tedious task.
    - All issues related to high availability, failures, failures on restart, and reliability were therefore a core requirement for YARN.
- Backward compatibility:
    - Hadoop 1.x has been in the picture for a while, with many successful production deployments across many industries. This massive installation base of MapReduce applications and the ecosystem of related projects, such as Hive, Pig, and so on, would not tolerate a radical redesign. Therefore, the new architecture reused as much code from the existing framework as possible, and no major surgery was conducted on it. This made MRv2 able to ensure satisfactory compatibility with MRv1 applications.

Summary

In this chapter, you learned what YARN is and how it has turned out to be the modern operating system for Hadoop, making it a multiapplication platform.

In *Chapter 2, YARN Architecture*, we will be talking about the architecture details of YARN.

2
YARN Architecture

This chapter dives deep into YARN architecture its core components, and how they interact to deliver optimal resource utilization, better performance, and manageability. It also focuses on some important terminology concerning YARN.

In this chapter, we will cover the following topics:

- Core components of YARN architecture
- Interaction and flow of YARN components
- ResourceManager scheduling policies
- Recent developments in YARN

The motivation behind the YARN architecture is to support more data processing models, such as Apache Spark, Apache Storm, Apache Giraph, Apache HAMA, and so on, than just MapReduce. YARN provides a platform to develop and execute distributed processing applications. It also improves efficiency and resource-sharing capabilities.

The design decision behind YARN architecture is to separate two major functionalities, resource management and job scheduling or monitoring of JobTracker, into separate daemons, that is, a cluster level **ResourceManager** (**RM**) and an application-specific **ApplicationMaster** (**AM**). YARN architecture follows a master-slave architectural model in which the ResourceManager is the master and node-specific slave **NodeManager** (**NM**). The global ResourceManager and per-node NodeManager builds a most generic, scalable, and simple platform for distributed application management. The ResourceManager is the supervisor component that manages the resources among the applications in the whole system. The per-application ApplicationMaster is the application-specific daemon that negotiates resources from ResourceManager and works in hand with NodeManagers to execute and monitor the application's tasks.

The following diagram explains how JobTracker is replaced by a global level ResourceManager and ApplicationManager and a per-node TaskTracker is replaced by an application-level ApplicationMaster to manage its functions and responsibilities. JobTracker and TaskTracker only support MapReduce applications with less scalability and poor cluster utilization. Now, YARN supports multiple distributed data processing models with improved scalability and cluster utilization.

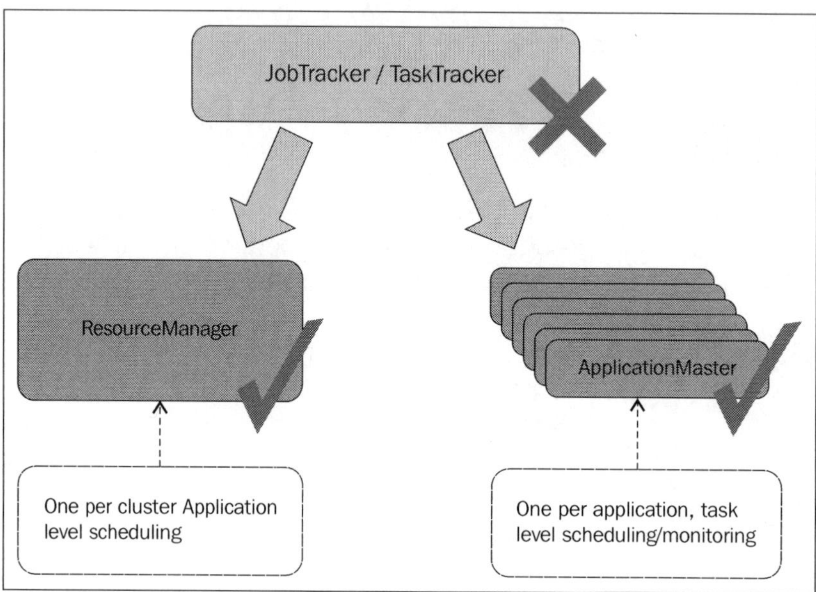

The ResourceManager has a cluster-level scheduler that has responsibility for resource allocation to all the running tasks as per the ApplicationManager's requests. The primary responsibility of the ResourceManager is to allocate resources to the application(s). The ResourceManager is not responsible for tracking the status of an application or monitoring tasks. Also, it doesn't guarantee restarting/balancing tasks in the case of application or hardware failure.

The application-level ApplicationMaster is responsible for negotiating resources from the ResourceManager on application submission, such as memory, CPU, disk, and so on. It is also responsible for tracking an application's status and monitoring application processes in coordination with the NodeManager.

Let's have a look at the high-level architecture of Hadoop 2.0. As you can see, more applications can be supported by YARN than just the MapReduce application. The key component of Hadoop 2 is YARN, for better cluster resource management, and the underlying file system remains the same as **Hadoop Distributed File System** (**HDFS**) and is shown in the following image:

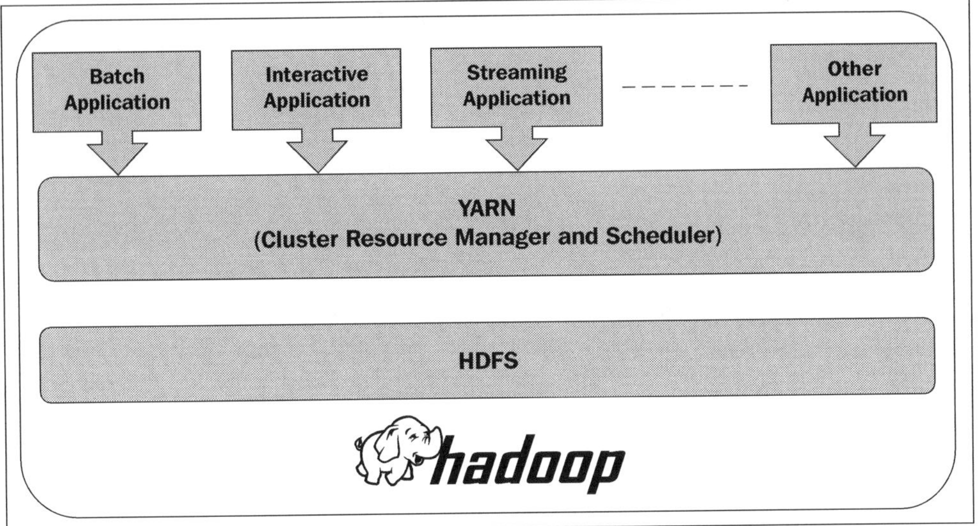

Here are some key concepts that we should know before exploring the YARN architecture in detail:

- **Application**: This is the job submitted to the framework, for example a MapReduce job. It could also be a shell script.
- **Container**: This is the basic unit of hardware allocation, for example a container that has 4 GB of RAM and one CPU. The container does optimized resource allocation; this replaces the fixed map and reduce slots in the previous versions of Hadoop.

Core components of YARN architecture

Here are some core components of YARN architecture that we need to know:

- ResourceManager
- ApplicationMaster
- NodeManager

ResourceManager

ResourceManager acts as a global resource scheduler that is responsible for resource management and scheduling as per the ApplicationMaster's requests for the resource requirements of the application(s). It is also responsible for the management of hierarchical job queues. The ResourceManager can be seen in the following figure:

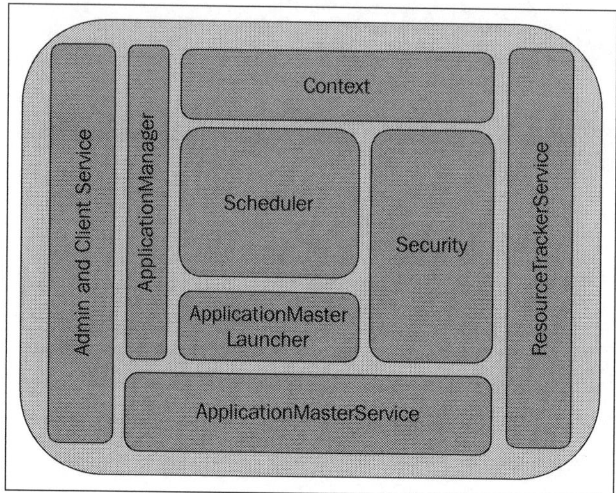

The preceding diagram gives more details about the components of the ResourceManager. The Admin and Client service is responsible for client interactions, such as a job request submission, start, restart, and so on. The **ApplicationsManager** is responsible for the management of every application. The **ApplicationMasterService** interacts with every application. ApplicationMaster regarding resource or container negotiation, the ResourceTrackerService coordinates with the NodeManager and ResourceManager. **The ApplicationMaster Launcher** service is responsible for launching a container for the ApplicationMaster on job submission from the client. The **Scheduler** and **Security** are the core parts of the ResourceManager. As already explained, the Scheduler is responsible for resource negotiation and allocation to the applications as per the request of the ApplicationMaster. There are three different policies of scheduler, FIFO, Fair, and Capacity, which will be explained in detail later in this chapter. The security component is responsible for generating and delegating an/the ApplicationToken and ContainerToken to access the application and container, respectively.

ApplicationMaster (AM)

The ApplicationMaster is at a per-application level. It is responsible for the application's life cycle management and for negotiating the appropriate resources from the Scheduler, tracking their status and progress monitoring, for example, MapReduce ApplicationMaster.

NodeManager (NM)

NodeManager acts as a per-machine agent and is responsible for managing the life cycle of the container and for monitoring their resource usage. The core components of the NodeManager are shown in the following diagram:

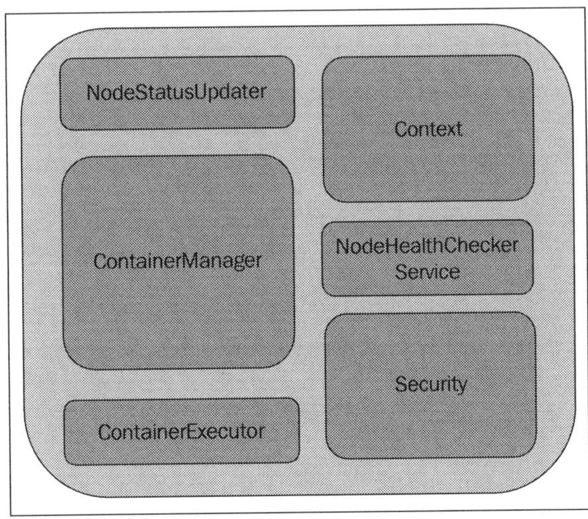

The component responsible for communication between the NodeManager and ResourceManager is the **NodeStatusUpdater**. The **ContainerManager** is the core component of the NodeManager; it manages all the containers that run on the node. **NodeHealthCheckerService** is the service that monitors the node's health and communicates the node's heartbeat to the ResourceManager via the NodeStatusUpdater service. The **ContainerExecutor** is the process responsible for interacting with native hardware or software to start or stop the container process. Management of **Access Control List** (**ACL**) and access token verification is performed by the **Security** component.

Let's take a look at one scenario to understand YARN architecture in detail. Refer to the following diagram:

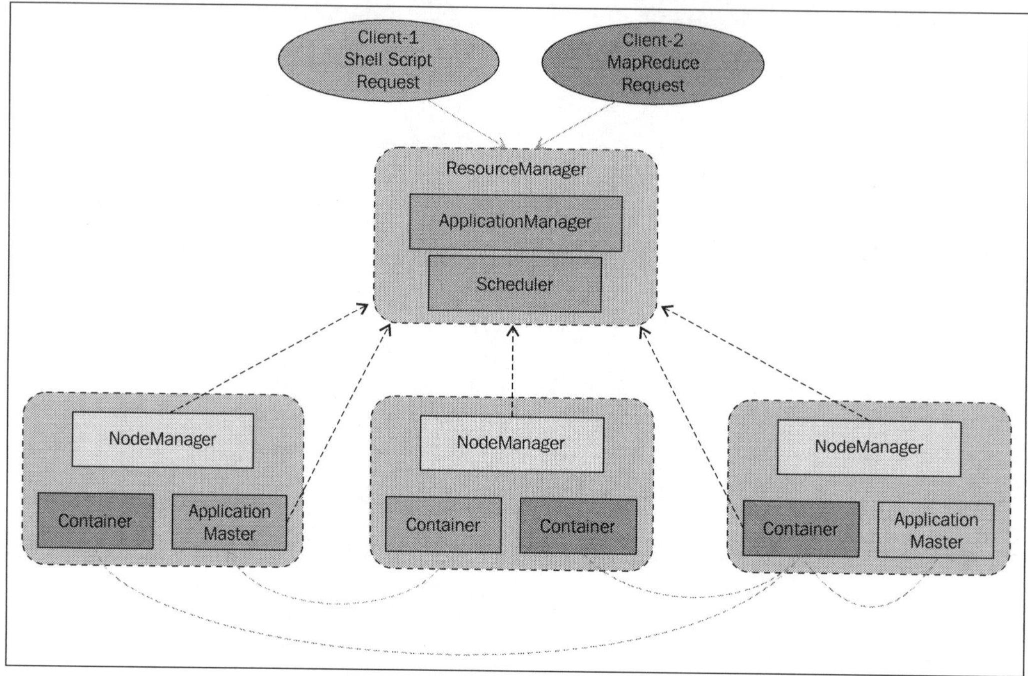

Say we have two client requests: one wants to execute a simple shell script, while another one wants to execute a complex MapReduce job. The Shell Script is represented in maroon color, while the MapReduce job is represented in light green color in the preceding diagram.

The ResourceManager has two main components, the ApplicationManager and the Scheduler. The ApplicationManager is responsible for accepting the client's job submission requests, negotiating the containers to execute the applications specific to the ApplicationMaster, and providing the services to restart the ApplicationMaster on failure. The responsibility of the Scheduler is to allocate resources to the various running applications with respect to the application resource requirements and available resources. The Scheduler is a pure scheduler in the sense that it provides no monitoring or tracking functions for the application. Also, it doesn't offer any guarantees for restarting a failed task either due to failure in the application or in the hardware. The Scheduler performs its scheduling tasks based on the resource requirements of the application(s); it does so based on the abstract notion of the resource container, which incorporates elements such as CPU, memory, disk, and so on.

The NodeManager is the per-machine framework daemon that is responsible for the containers' life cycles. It is also responsible for monitoring their resource usage, for example, memory, CPU, disk, network, and so on, and for reporting this to the ResourceManager accordingly. The application-level ApplicationMaster is responsible for negotiating the required resource containers from the scheduler, tracking their status, and monitoring progress. In the preceding diagram, you can see that both jobs, Shell Script and MapReduce, have an individual ApplicationMaster that allocates resources for job execution and to track/monitor the job execution status.

Now, take a look at the execution sequence of the application. Refer to the preceding application flow diagram.

A client submits the application to the ResourceManager. In the preceding diagram, client 1 submits a Shell Script Request (maroon color), and client 2 submits a MapReduce request (green color):

1. Then, the ResourceManager allocates a container to start up the ApplicationMaster as per the application submitted by the client: one ApplicationMaster for the shell script and one for the MapReduce application.
2. While starting the ApplicationMaster, the ResourceManager registers the application with the ResourceManager.
3. After the startup of the ApplicationMaster, it negotiates with the ResourceManager for appropriate resources as per the application requirement.
4. Then, after resource allocation from the ResourceManager, the ApplicationMaster requests that the NodeManager launches the containers allocated by the ResourceManager.
5. On successful launching of the containers, the application code executes within the container, and the ApplicationManager reports back to the ResourceManager with the execution status of the application.
6. During the execution of the application, the client can request the ApplicationMaster or the ResourceManager directly for the application status, progress updates, and so on.
7. On execution of the application, the ApplicationMaster requests that the ResourceManager unregisters and shut downs its own container process.

YARN scheduler policies

As explained in the previous section, the ResourceManager acts as a pluggable global scheduler that manages and controls all the containers (resources). There are three different policies that can be applied over the scheduler, as per requirements and resource availability. They are as follows:

- The FIFO scheduler
- The Fair scheduler
- The Capacity scheduler

The FIFO (First In First Out) scheduler

FIFO means First In First Out. As the name indicates, the job submitted first will get priority to execute; in other words, the job runs in the order of submission. FIFO is a queue-based scheduler. It is a very simple approach to scheduling and it does not guarantee performance efficiency, as each job would use a whole cluster for execution. So other jobs may keep waiting to finish their execution, although a shared cluster has a great capability to offer more-than-enough resources to many users.

The fair scheduler

Fair scheduling is the policy of scheduling that assigns resources for the execution of the application so that all applications get an equal share of cluster recourses over a period of time. For example, if a single job is running, it would get all the resources available in the cluster, and as the job number increases, free recourses will be given to the jobs so that each user will get a fair share of the cluster. If two users have submitted two different jobs, a short job that belongs to a user would complete in a small timespan while a longer job submitted by the other user keeps running, so long jobs will still make some progress.

In a Fair scheduling policy, all jobs are placed into job pools, specific to users; accordingly, each user gets their own job pool. The user who submits more jobs than the other user will not get more resources than the first user on average. You may even define your own customized job pools with specified configurations. Fair scheduling is a preemptive scheduling, as if a pool has not received fair resources to run a particular task for a certain period of time. In this case, the scheduler will kill the tasks in pools that run out of capacity, to release resources to the pools that run under capacity.

In addition to fair scheduling, the Fair scheduler allocates a guaranteed minimum share of resources to the pools. This is always helpful for the users, groups, or applications, as they always get sufficient resources for execution.

The capacity scheduler

The Capacity scheduler is designed to allow applications to share cluster resources in a predictable and simple fashion. These are commonly known as "job queues". The main idea behind capacity scheduling is to allocate available resources to the running applications, based on individual needs and requirements. There are additional benefits when running the application using capacity scheduling, as they can access the excess capacity resources that are not being used by any other applications.

The abstraction provided by the capacity scheduler is the queue. It provides capacity guarantees for support for multiple queues where a job is submitted to the queue, and queues are allocated a capacity in the sense that a certain capacity of resources will be at their disposal. All the jobs submitted to the queue will access the resources allocated to the job queue. Admins can control the capacity of each queue.

Here are some basic features of the capacity scheduler:

- **Security**: Each queue has strict ACLs that take control of the authorization and authentication of users who can submit jobs to individual queues.
- **Elasticity**: Free resources are allocated to any queue beyond its capacity. If there is demand for these resources from queues that run below capacity, then as soon as the task scheduled on these resources has completed, they will be assigned to jobs on queues that run under capacity.
- **Operability**: The admin can, at any point in time, change queue definitions and properties.
- **Multitenancy**: All sets of limits are provided to prevent a single job, user, and queue from obtaining the resources of the queue or cluster. This is to ensure that the system, specifically a previous version of Hadoop, is not suppressed by too many tasks.
- **Resource-based scheduling:** Intensive job support, as jobs can specifically demand for higher resource requirements than default.
- **Job priorities**: These job queues can support job priorities. Within the queue, jobs with high priority have access to resources before jobs with lower priority.

Recent developments in YARN architecture

The ResourceManager is a single point of failure and restart because of various reasons: bugs, hardware failure, deliberate downtime for upgrading, and so on.

We already saw how crucial the role of the ResourceManager in YARN architecture is. The ResourceManager has become a single point of failure; if the ResourceManager in a cluster goes down, everything on that cluster will be lost.

So in a recent development of YARN, ResourceManager HA became a high priority. This recent development of YARN not only covers ResourceManager HA, but also provides transparency to users and does not require them to monitor such events explicitly and resubmit the jobs.

Overly complex in MRv1 for the fact that JobTracker has to save too much of meta-data: both cluster state and per-application running state. This means that if Job-Tracker dies, then all the applications in a running state will be lost.

The development of ResourceManager recovery will be done in two phases:

1. RM Restart Phase I: In this phase, all the applications will be killed while restarting the ResourceManager on failure. No state of the application can be stored. Development of this phase is almost completed.
2. RM Restart Phase II: As in Phase II, the application will store the state on RM failure; this means that applications are not killed, and they report the running state back to the RM after the RM comes back up.

The ResourceManager will be used only to save an application's submission metadata and cluster-level information. Application state persistence and the recovery of specific information will be managed by the application itself.

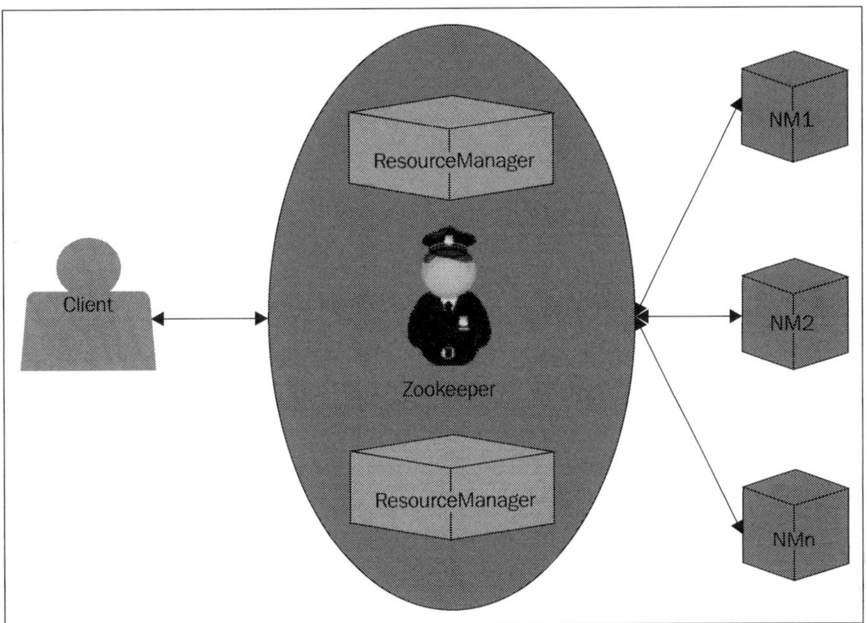

As shown in the preceding diagram, in the next version, we will get a pluggable state store, such as Zookeeper and HDFS, that can store the state of the running applications. ResourceManager HA would contain synchronized active-passive ResourceManager architectural models managed by Zookeeper; as one goes down, the other can take over cluster responsibility without halting and losing information.

Summary

In this chapter, we covered the architectural components of YARN, their responsibilities, and their interoperations. We also focused on some major development work going on in the community to overcome the drawbacks of the current release. In the next chapter, we will cover the installation steps of YARN.

3
YARN Installation

In this section, we'll cover the installation of Hadoop and YARN and their configuration for a single-node and single-cluster setup. Now, we will consider Hadoop as two different components: one is **Hadoop Distributed File System (HDFS)**, the other is YARN. The YARN components take care of resource allocation and the scheduling of the jobs that run over the data stored in HDFS. We'll cover most of the configurations to make YARN distributed computing more optimized and efficient.

In this chapter, we will cover the following topics:

- Hadoop and YARN single-node installation
- Hadoop and YARN fully-distributed mode installation
- Operating Hadoop and YARN clusters

Single-node installation

Let's start with the steps for Hadoop's single-node installations, as it's easy to understand and set up. This way, we can quickly perform simple operations using Hadoop MapReduce and the HDFS.

Prerequisites

Here are some prerequisites needed for Hadoop installations; make sure that the prerequisites are fulfilled to start working with Hadoop and YARN.

Platform

GNU/Unix is supported for Hadoop installation as a development as well as a production platform. The Windows platform is also supported for Hadoop installation, with some extra configurations. Now, we'll focus more on Linux-based platforms, as Hadoop is more widely used with these platforms and works more efficiently with Linux compared to Windows systems. Here are the steps for single-node Hadoop installation for Linux systems. If you want to install it on Windows, refer to the Hadoop wiki page for the installation steps.

Software

Here's some software; make sure that they are installed before installing Hadoop.

Java must be installed. Confirm whether the Java version is compatible with the Hadoop version that is to be installed by checking the Hadoop wiki page (`http://wiki.apache.org/hadoop/HadoopJavaVersions`).

SSH and SSHD must be installed and running, as they are used by Hadoop scripts to manage remote Hadoop daemons.

Now, download the recent stable release of the Hadoop distribution from Apache mirrors and archives using the following command:

```
$$ wget http://mirrors.ibiblio.org/apache/hadoop/common/hadoop-2.6.0/
hadoop-2.6.0.tar.gz
```

Note that at the time of writing this book, Hadoop 2.6.0 is the most recent stable release. Now use the following commands:

```
$$ mkdir -p /opt/yarn
$$ cd /opt/yarn
$$ tar xvzf /root/hadoop-2.6.0.tar.gz
```

Starting with the installation

Now, unzip the download distribution under the `/etc/` directory. Change the Hadoop environmental parameters as per the following configurations.

Set the JAVA_HOME environmental parameter to the JAVA root installed before:

```
$$ export JAVA_HOME=etc/java/latest
```

Set the Hadoop home to the Hadoop installation directory:

```
$$ export HADOOP_HOME=etc/hadoop
```

Try running the Hadoop command. It should display the Hadoop documentation; this indicates a successful Hadoop configuration.

Now, our Hadoop single-node setup is ready to run in the following modes.

The standalone mode (local mode)

By default, Hadoop runs in standalone mode as a single Java process. This mode is useful for development and debugging.

The pseudo-distributed mode

Hadoop can run on a single node in pseudo-distributed mode, as each daemon is run as a separate Java process. To run Hadoop in pseudo-distributed mode, follow these configuration instructions. First, navigate to the `/etc/hadoop/core-site.xml`.

This configuration for the NameNode setup will run on localhost port `9000`. You can set the following property for the NameNode:

```
<configuration>
    <property>
        <name>fs.defaultFS</name>
        <value>hdfs://localhost:9000</value>
    </property>
</configuration>
```

Now navigate to `/etc/hadoop/hdfs-site.xml`.

By setting the following property, we are ensuring that the replication factor of each data block is 3 (by default, the replication factor is 3):

```
<configuration>
    <property>
        <name>dfs.replication</name>
        <value>3</value>
    </property>
</configuration>
```

Then, format the Hadoop filesystem using this command:

```
$$ $HADOOP_HOME/bin/hdfs namenode -format
```

After formatting the filesystem, start the namenode and datanode daemons using the next command. You can see logs under the `$HADOOP_HOME/logs` directory by default:

```
$$ $HADOOP_HOME/sbin/start-dfs.sh
```

Now, we can see the namenode UI on the web interface. Hit `http://localhost:50070/` in the browser.

Create the HDFS directories that are required to run MapReduce jobs:

```
$$ $HADOOP_HOME/bin/hdfs -mkdir /user
$$ $HADOOP_HOME/bin/hdfs -mkdir /user/{username}
```

To MapReduce job on YARN in pseudo-distributed mode, you need to start the ResourceManager and NodeManager daemons. Navigate to `/etc/hadoop/mapred-site.xml`:

```
<configuration>
    <property>
        <name>mapreduce.framework.name</name>
        <value>yarn</value>
    </property>
</configuration>
```

Navigate to `/etc/hadoop/yarn-site.xml`:

```
<configuration>
    <property>
        <name>yarn.nodemanager.aux-services</name>
        <value>mapreduce_shuffle</value>
    </property>
</configuration>
```

Now, start the ResourceManager and NodeManager daemons by issuing this command:

```
$$ sbin/start-yarn.sh
```

By simply navigating to `http://localhost:8088/` in your browser, you can see the web interface for the ResourceManager. From here, you can start, restart, or stop the jobs.

To stop the YARN daemons, you need to run the following command:

```
$$ $HADOOP_HOME/sbin/stop-yarn.sh
```

This is how we can configure Hadoop and YARN in a single node in standalone and pseudo-distributed modes. Moving forward, we will focus on fully-distributed mode. As the basic configuration remains the same, we only need to do some extra configuration for fully-distributed mode. Single-node setup is mainly used for development and debugging of distributed applications, while fully-distributed mode is used for the production setup.

The fully-distributed mode

In the previous section, we highlighted the standalone Hadoop and YARN configurations, and in this section we'll focus on the fully-distributed mode setup. This section describes how to install, configure, and manage Hadoop and YARN in fully-distributed, very large clusters with thousands of nodes in them.

In order to start with fully-distributed mode, we first need to download the stable version of Hadoop from Apache mirrors. Installing Hadoop in distributed mode generally means unpacking the software distribution on each machine in the cluster or installing **Red Hat Package Managers** (**RPMs**). As Hadoop follows a master-slave architecture, one machine in the cluster is designated as the **NameNode** (**NN**), one as the **ResourceManager** (**RM**), and the rest of the machines, **DataNodes** (**DN**) and **NodeManagers** (**NM**), will typically acts as slaves.

After the successful unpacking of software distribution on each cluster machine or RPM installation, you need to take care of a very important part of the Hadoop installation phase, Hadoop configuration.

Hadoop typically has two types of configuration: one is the read-only default configuration (`core-default.xml`, `hdfs-default.xml`, `yarn-default.xml`, and `mapred-default.xml`), while the other is the site-specific configuration (`core-site.xml`, `hdfs-site.xml`, `yarn-site.xml`, and `mapred-site.xml`). All these file are found under the `$HADOOP_HOME/conf` directory.

In addition to the preceding configuration files, the Hadoop-environment and YARN-environment specific file is found in `conf/hadoop-env.sh` and `conf/yarn-env.sh`. As for the Hadoop and YARN cluster configuration, you need to set up an environment in which Hadoop daemons can execute. The Hadoop/YARN daemons are the NameNode/ResourceManager (masters) and the DataNode/NodeManager (slaves).

First, make sure that JAVA_HOME is correctly specified on each node.

Here are some important configuration parameters with respect to each daemon:

- **NameNode**: HADOOP_NAMENODE_OPTS
- **DataNode**: HADOOP_DATANODE_OPTS
- **Secondary NameNode**: HADOOP_SECONDARYNAMENODE_OPTS
- **ResourceManager**: YARN_RESOURCEMANAGER_OPTS
- **NodeManager**: YARN_NODEMANAGER_OPTS
- **WebAppProxy**: YARN_PROXYSERVER_OPTS
- **Map Reduce Job History Server**: HADOOP_JOB_HISTORYSERVER_OPTS

For example, to run the NameNode in parallelGC mode, the following line should be added into `hadoop-env.sh`:

```
$$ export HADOOP_NAMENODE_OPTS="-XX:+UseParallelGC ${HADOOP_NAMENODE_
OPTS}"
```

Here are some important configuration parameters with respect to the daemon and its configuration files.

Navigate to `conf/core-site.xml` and configure it as follows:

```
fs.defaultFS: NameNode URI, hdfs://<hdfshost>:<hdfsport>
  <property>
     <name>fs.defaultFS</name>
     <value>hdfs://$<hdfshostname>:<hdfsport></value>
     <description>It is a NameNode hostname</description>
  </property>
```

The io.file.buffer.size: 4096, read and write buffer size of files.

The buffer size for I/O (read/write) operation on sequence files stored in disk files, that is, it determines how much data is buffered in I/O pipes before transferring it to other operations during read/write operations. I should be multiple of OS filesystem block size.

```
<property>
 <name>io.file.buffer.size</name>
 <value>4096</value>
 <description>read and write buffer size of files</description>
</property>
```

Now navigate to `conf/hdfs-site.xml`. Here is the configuration for the NameNode:

Parameter	**Description**
`dfs.namenode.name.dir`	The path on the local filesystem where the NameNode generates the namespace and application transaction logs.
`dfs.namenode.hosts`	The list of permitted DataNodes.
`dfs.namenode.hosts.exclude`	The list of excluded DataNodes.
`dfs.blocksize`	The default value is 268435456. The HDFS block size is 256 MB for large filesystems.
`dfs.namenode.handler.count`	The default value is 100. More NameNode server threads to handle RPCs from a large number of DataNodes.

The configuration for the DataNode is as follows:

Parameter	**Description**
`dfs.datanode.data.dir`	Comma-delimited list of paths on the local filesystems where the DataNode stores the blocks

Now navigate to `conf/yarn-site.xml`. We'll take a look at the configurations related to the ResourceManager and NodeManager:

Parameter	Description
`yarn.acl.enable`	Values are `true` or `false` to enable or disable ACLs. The default value is false.
`yarn.admin.acl`	This refers to the admin or ACL. The default is `*`, which means anyone can do admin tasks. ACL sets admins on the cluster. This could be a comma-delimited user group to set more than one admin.
`yarn.log-aggregation-enable`	This is `true` or `false` to enable or disable log aggregation.

Now, we will take look at configurations for the ResourceManager in the `conf/yarn-site.xml` file:

Parameter	Description
`yarn.resourcemanager.address`	This is the ResourceManager host:port for clients to submit jobs.
`yarn.resourcemanager.scheduler.address`	This is the ResourceManager host:port for ApplicationMasters to talk to the Scheduler to obtain resources.
`yarn.resourcemanager.resource-tracker.address`	This is the ResourceManager host:port for NodeManagers.
`yarn.resourcemanager.admin.address`	This is the ResourceManager host:port for administrative commands.
`yarn.resourcemanager.webapp.address`	This is the ResourceManager web-ui host:port.
`yarn.resourcemanager.scheduler.class`	This is the ResourceManager Scheduler class. The values are CapacityScheduler, FairScheduler, and FifoScheduler.
`yarn.scheduler.minimum-allocation-mb`	This is the minimum limit of memory to allocate to each container request in the Resource Manager.
`yarn.scheduler.maximum-allocation-mb`	This is the maximum limit of memory to allocate to each container request in the Resource Manager.

Parameter	Description
`yarn.resourcemanager.nodes.include-path/ yarn.resourcemanager.nodes.exclude-path`	This is the list of permitted/excluded NodeManagers. If necessary, use these files to control the list of permitted NodeManagers.

Now take look at configurations for the NodeManager in `conf/yarn-site.xml`:

Parameter	Description
`yarn.nodemanager.resource.memory-mb`	This refers to the available physical memory (MBs) for the NodeManager. It defines the total available memory resources on the NodeManager to be made available to the running containers.
`yarn.nodemanager.vmem-pmem-ratio`	This refers to the maximum ratio by which virtual memory usage of tasks may exceed physical memory.
`yarn.nodemanager.local-dirs`	This refers to the list of directory paths on the local filesystem where intermediate data is written. This should be a comma-separated list.
`yarn.nodemanager.log-dirs`	This refers to the path on the local filesystem where logs are written.
`yarn.nodemanager.log.retain-seconds`	This refers to the time (in seconds) to persist logfiles on the NodeManager. The default value is 10800 seconds. This configuration is applicable only if log aggregation is enabled.
`yarn.nodemanager.remote-app-log-dir`	This is the HDFS directory path to which logs have been moved after application completion. The default path is `/logs`. This configuration is applicable only if log aggregation is enabled.
`yarn.nodemanager.remote-app-log-dir-suffix`	This refers to the specified suffix appended to the remote log directory. This configuration is applicable only if log aggregation is enabled.
`yarn.nodemanager.aux-services`	This refers to the shuffle service that specifically needs to be set for MapReduce applications.

HistoryServer

The HistoryServer allows all YARN applications with a central location to aggregate their completed jobs for historical reference and debugging. The settings for the MapReduce JobHistoryServer can be found in the `mapred-default.xml` file:

- `mapreduce.jobhistory.address`: MapReduce JobHistory Server host:port. The default port is `10020`.
- `mapreduce.jobhistory.webapp.address`: This is the MapReduce JobHistory Server Web UI host:port. The default port is `19888`.
- `mapreduce.jobhistory.intermediate-done-dir`: This is the directory where history files are written by MapReduce jobs (in HDFS). The default is `/mr-history/tmp`.
- `mapreduce.jobhistory.done-dir`: This is the directory where history files are managed by the MR JobHistory Server (in HDFS). The default is `/mr-history/done`.

Slave files

With respect to the Hadoop slave and YARN slave nodes, generally one chooses one node in the cluster as the NameNode (Hadoop master), another node as the ResourceManager (YARN master), and the rest of the machine acts as both Hadoop slave DataNodes and Yarn slave NodeManagers. List all the slaves, one per line hostname or IP addresses in your Hadoop `conf/slaves` file.

Operating Hadoop and YARN clusters

This is the final stage of Hadoop and YARN cluster setup and configuration. Here are the commands that need to be used to start and stop the Hadoop and YARN clusters.

Starting Hadoop and YARN clusters

To start Hadoop and the YARN cluster, use with the following procedure:

1. Format a Hadoop distributed filesystem:

   ```
   $HADOOP_HOME/bin/hdfs namenode -format <cluster_name>
   ```

2. The following command is used to start HDFS. Run it on the NameNode:
   ```
   $HADOOP_HOME/sbin/hadoop-daemon.sh --config $HADOOP_CONF_DIR
   --script hdfs start namenode
   ```
3. Run this command to start DataNodes on all slaves nodes:
   ```
   $HADOOP_HOME/sbin/hadoop-daemon.sh --config $HADOOP_CONF_DIR
   --script hdfs start datanode
   ```
4. Start YARN with the following command on the ResourceManager:
   ```
   $HADOOP_YARN_HOME/sbin/yarn-daemon.sh --config $HADOOP_CONF_DIR
   start resourcemanager
   ```
5. Execute this command to start NodeManagers on all slaves:
   ```
   $HADOOP_YARN_HOME/sbin/yarn-daemon.sh --config $HADOOP_CONF_DIR
   start nodemanager
   ```
6. Start a standalone WebAppProxy server. This is used for load-balancing purposes on a multiserver cluster:
   ```
   $HADOOP_YARN_HOME/sbin/yarn-daemonart proxyserver --config
   $HADOOP_CONF_DIR
   ```
7. Execute this command on the designated HistoryServer:
   ```
   $HADOOP_HOME/sbin/mr-jobhistory-daemon.sh start historyserver
   --config $HADOOP_CONF_DIR
   ```

Stopping Hadoop and YARN clusters

To stop Hadoop and the YARN cluster, use with the following procedure:

1. Use the following command on the NameNode to stop it:
   ```
   $HADOOP_HOME/sbin/hadoop-daemon.sh --config $HADOOP_CONF_DIR
   --script hdfs stop namenode
   ```
2. Issue this command on all the slave nodes to stop DataNodes:
   ```
   $HADOOP_HOME/sbin/hadoop-daemon.sh --config $HADOOP_CONF_DIR
   --script hdfs stop datanode
   ```
3. To stop the ResourceManager, issue the following command on the specified ResourceManager:
   ```
   $HADOOP_YARN_HOME/sbin/yarn-daemon.sh --config $HADOOP_CONF_DIR
   stop resourcemanager
   ```

4. The following command is used to stop the NodeManager on all slave nodes:

```
$HADOOP_YARN_HOME/sbin/yarn-daemon.sh --config $HADOOP_CONF_DIR
stop nodemanager
```

5. Stop the WebAppProxy server:

```
$HADOOP_YARN_HOME/sbin/yarn-daemon.sh stop proxyserver --config
$HADOOP_CONF_DIR
```

6. Stop the MapReduce JobHistory Server by running the following command on the HistoryServer:

```
$HADOOP_HOME/sbin/mr-jobhistory-daemon.sh stop historyserver
--config $HADOOP_CONF_DIR
```

Web interfaces of the Ecosystem

It's all about the Hadoop and YARN setup and configurations and commanding over Hadoop and YARN. Here are some web interfaces used by Hadoop and YARN administrators for admin tasks:

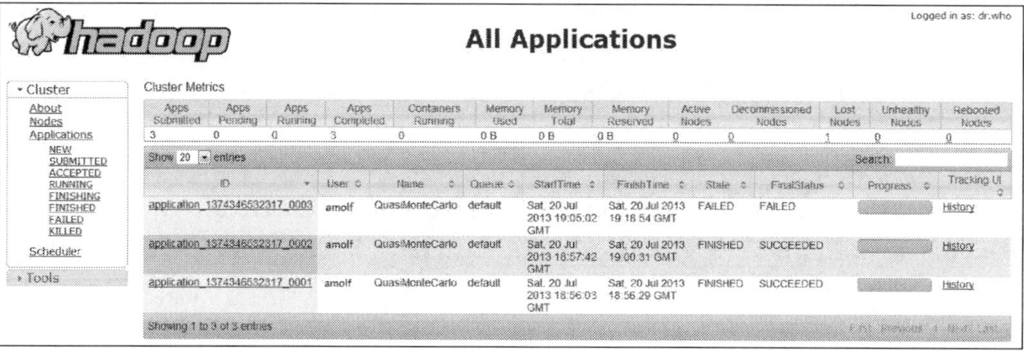

The URL for the NameNode is `http://<namenode_host>:<port>/` and the default HTTP port is `50070`.

The URL for the ResourceManager is http://<resourcermanager_host>:<port>/ and the default HTTP port is 8088. TheWeb UI for the NameNode can be seen as follows:

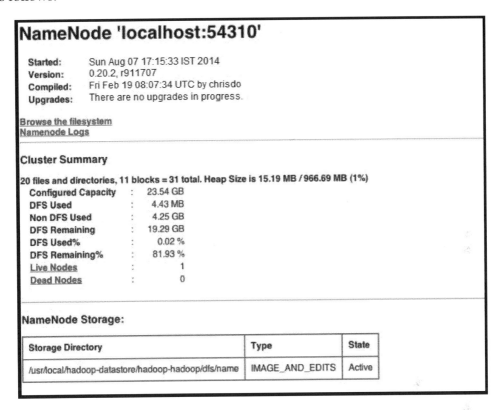

NameNode 'localhost:54310'

Started:	Sun Aug 07 17:15:33 IST 2014
Version:	0.20.2, r911707
Compiled:	Fri Feb 19 08:07:34 UTC by chrisdo
Upgrades:	There are no upgrades in progress.

Browse the filesystem
Namenode Logs

Cluster Summary

20 files and directories, 11 blocks = 31 total. Heap Size is 15.19 MB / 966.69 MB (1%)

Configured Capacity	:	23.54 GB
DFS Used	:	4.43 MB
Non DFS Used	:	4.25 GB
DFS Remaining	:	19.29 GB
DFS Used%	:	0.02 %
DFS Remaining%	:	81.93 %
Live Nodes	:	1
Dead Nodes	:	0

NameNode Storage:

Storage Directory	Type	State
/usr/local/hadoop-datastore/hadoop-hadoop/dfs/name	IMAGE_AND_EDITS	Active

The URL for the MapReduce JobHistory Server is http://<jobhistoryserver_host>:<port>/ and the default HTTP port is 19888.

Summary

In this section, we covered Hadoop and YARN single-node and fully-distributed cluster setup and important configurations. We also covered the basic but important commands to administrate Hadoop and YARN clusters. In the next chapter, we'll look at the Hadoop and YARN components in more detail.

4
YARN and Hadoop Ecosystems

This chapter discusses YARN with respect to Hadoop, since it is very important to know where exactly YARN fits in Hadoop 2 now.

Hadoop 2 has undergone a complete change in terms of architecture and components compared to Hadoop 1.

In this chapter, we will be cover the following topics:

- A short introduction to Hadoop 1
- The difference between MRv1 and MRv2
- Where YARN fits in Hadoop 2
- Old and new MapReduce APIs
- Backward compatibility of MRv2 APIs
- Practical examples of MRv1 and MRv2

The Hadoop 2 release

YARN came into the picture with the release of Hadoop 0.23 on November 11, 2011. This was the alpha version of the Hadoop 0.23 major release.

The major difference between 0.23 and pre-0.23 releases is that the 0.23 release had undergone a complete revamp in terms of the MapReduce engine and resource management. This 0.23 release separated out resource management and application life cycle management.

A short introduction to Hadoop 1.x and MRv1

We will briefly look at the basic Apache Hadoop 1.x and its processing framework, MRv1 (**Classic**), so that we can get a clear picture of the differences in Apache Hadoop 2.x MRv2 (**YARN**) in terms of architecture, components, and processing framework.

Apache Hadoop is a scalable, fault-tolerant distributed system for data storage and processing. The core programming model in Hadoop is MapReduce.

Since 2004, Hadoop has emerged as the de facto standard to store, process, and analyze hundreds of terabytes and even petabytes of data.

The major components in Hadoop 1.x are as follows:

- **NameNode**: This keeps the metadata in the main memory.
- **DataNode**: This is where the data resides in the form of blocks.
- **JobTracker**: This assigns/reassigns MapReduce tasks to TaskTrackers in the cluster and tracks the status of each TaskTracker.
- **TaskTracker**: This executes the task assigned by the JobTracker and sends the status of the task to the JobTracker.

The major components of Hadoop 1.x can be seen as follows:

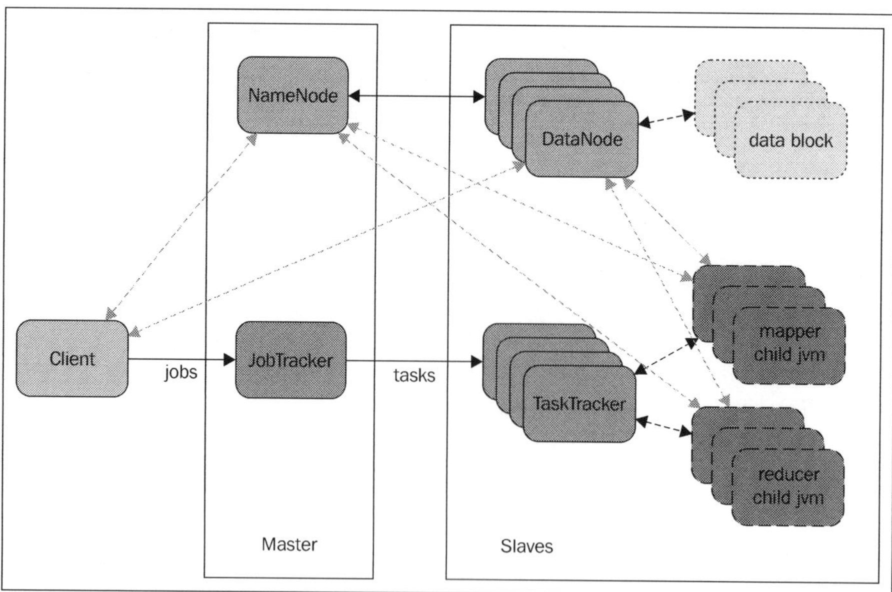

A typical Hadoop 1.x cluster (shown in the preceding figure) can consist of thousands of nodes. It follows the Master\Slave pattern, where the NameNodes\JobTrackers are the masters and the DataNodes\TaskTrackers are the slaves.

The main data processing is distributed across the cluster in the DataNodes to increase parallel processing.

The master NameNode process (master for slave DataNodes) manages the filesystem, and the master JobTracker process (master for slave TaskTrackers) manages the tasks. The topology is seen as follows:

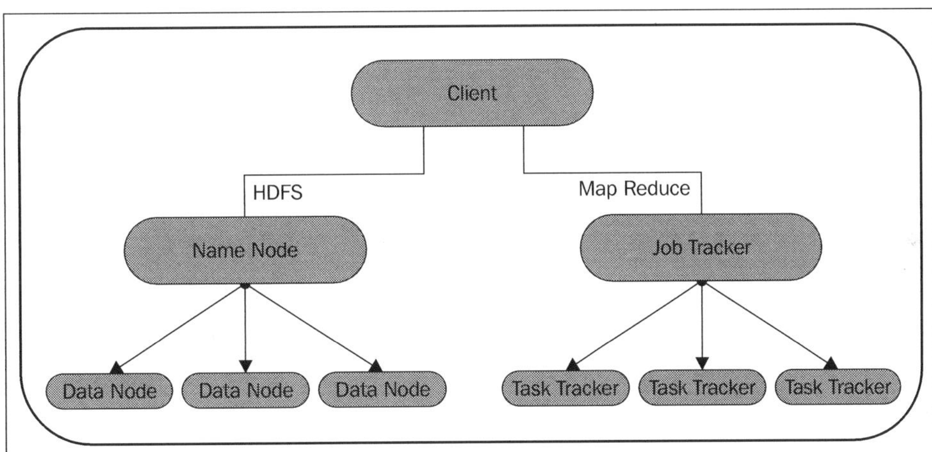

A Hadoop cluster can be considered to be mainly made up of two distinguishable parts:

- **HDFS**: This is the underlying storage layer that acts as a filesystem for distributed data storage. You can put data of any format, schema, and type on it, such as structured, semi-structured, or unstructured data. This flexibility makes Hadoop fit for the data lake, which is sometimes called the bit bucket or the landing zone.
- **MapReduce**: This is the execution layer which is the only distributed data-processing framework.

Downloading the example code

You can download the example code files from your account at `http://www.packtpub.com` for all the Packt Publishing books you have purchased. If you purchased this book elsewhere, you can visit `http://www.packtpub.com/support` and register to have the files e-mailed directly to you.

MRv1 versus MRv2

MRv1 (MapReduce version 1) is part of Apache Hadoop 1.x and is an implementation of the MapReduce programming paradigm.

The MapReduce project itself can be broken into the following parts:

- **End-user MapReduce API**: This is the API needed to develop the MapReduce application.
- **MapReduce framework**: This is the runtime implementation of various phases, such as the map phase, the sort/shuffle/merge aggregation phase, and the reduce phase.
- **MapReduce system**: This is the backend infrastructure required to run MapReduce applications and includes things such as cluster resource management, scheduling of jobs, and so on.

Hadoop 1.x was written solely as an MR engine. Since it runs on a cluster, its cluster management component was also tightly coupled with the MR programming paradigm. The *only* thing that could be run on Hadoop 1.x was an MR job.

In MRv1, the cluster was managed by a single JobTracker and multiple TaskTrackers running on the DataNodes.

In Hadoop 2.x, the old MRv1 framework was rewritten to run on top of YARN. This application was named MRv2, or MapReduce version 2. It is the familiar MapReduce execution underneath, except that each job now runs on YARN.

The core difference between MRv1 and MRv2 is the way the MapReduce jobs are executed.

With Hadoop 1.x, it was the JobTracker and TaskTrackers, but now with YARN on Hadoop 2.x, it's the ResourceManager, ApplicationMaster, and NodeManagers.

However, the underlying concept, the **MapReduce framework**, remains the same.

Hadoop 2 has been redefined from HDFS-plus-MapReduce to HDFS-plus-YARN.

Referring to the following figure, YARN took control of the resource management and application life cycle part of Hadoop 1.x.

YARN therefore, definitely results in increased ROI for Hadoop investment, in the sense that now the same Hadoop 2.x cluster resources can be used to do multiple things, such as batch processing, real-time processing, SQL applications, and so on.

Earlier, running this variety of applications was not possible, and people had to use a separate Hadoop cluster for MapReduce and a separate one to do something else.

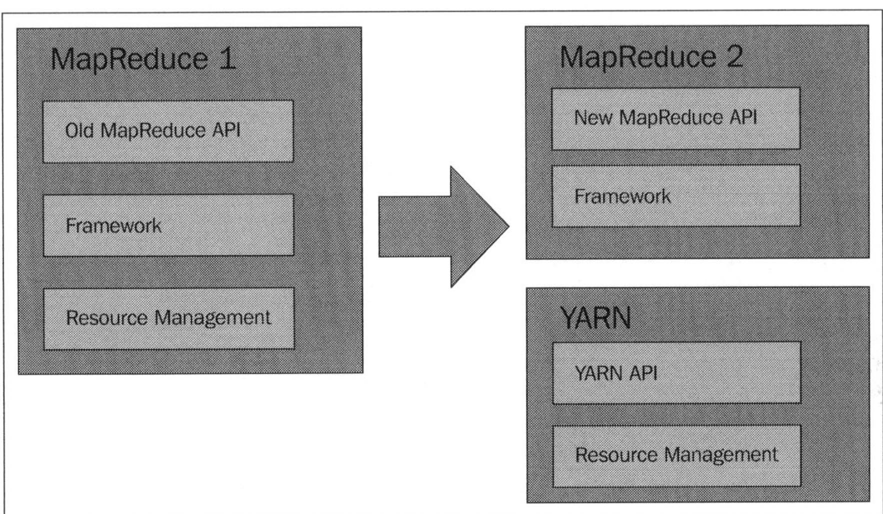

Understanding where YARN fits into Hadoop

If we refer to Hadoop 1.x in the first figure of this chapter, then it is clear that the responsibilities of the JobTracker mainly included the following:

- Managing the computational resources in terms of map and reduce slots
- Scheduling submitted jobs
- Monitoring the executions of the TaskTrackers
- Restarting failed tasks
- Performing a speculative execution of tasks
- Calculating the Job Counters

Clearly, the JobTracker alone does a lot of tasks together and is overloaded with lots of work.

This overloading of the JobTracker led to the **redesign of the JobTracker**, and YARN tried to reduce the responsibilities of the JobTracker in the following ways:

- Cluster resource management and Scheduling responsibilities were moved to the global **Resource Manager** (**RM**)
- The application life cycle management, that is, job execution and monitoring was moved into a per-application **ApplicationMaster** (**AM**)

The Global Resource Manager is seen in the following image:

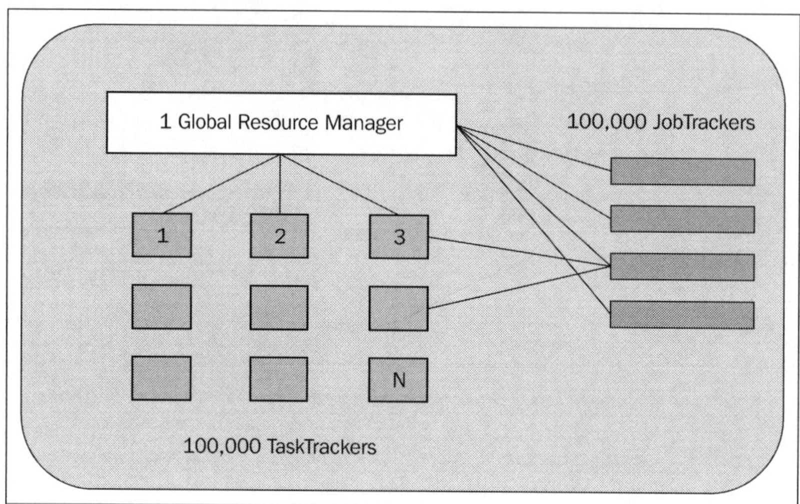

If you look at the preceding figure, you will clearly see the disappearance of the single centralized JobTracker; its place is taken by a Global Resource Manager.

Also, for each job a tiny, dedicated JobTracker is created, which monitors the tasks specific to its job. This tiny JobTracker is run on the slave node.

This tiny, dedicated JobTracker is termed an ApplicationMaster in the new framework (refer to the following figure).

Also, the TaskTrackers are referred to as NodeManagers in the new framework.

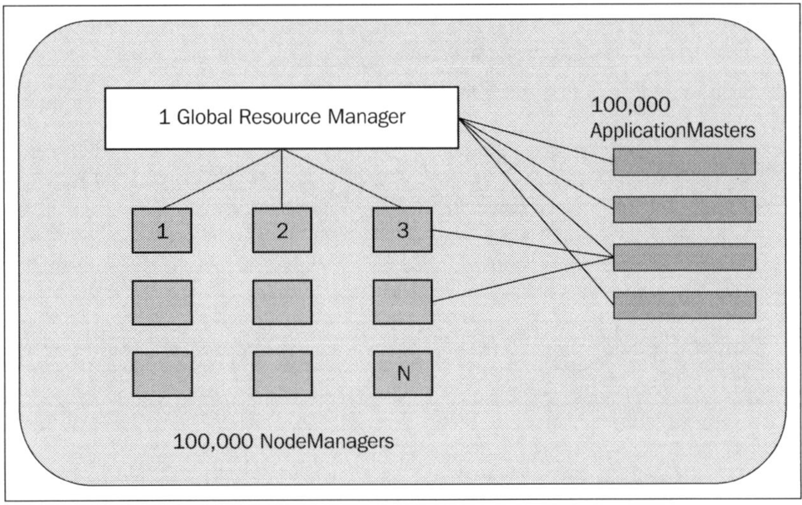

Finally, looking at the JobTracker redesign (in the following figure), we can clearly see that the JobTracker's responsibilities are broken into a per-cluster ResourceManager and a per-application ApplicationMaster:

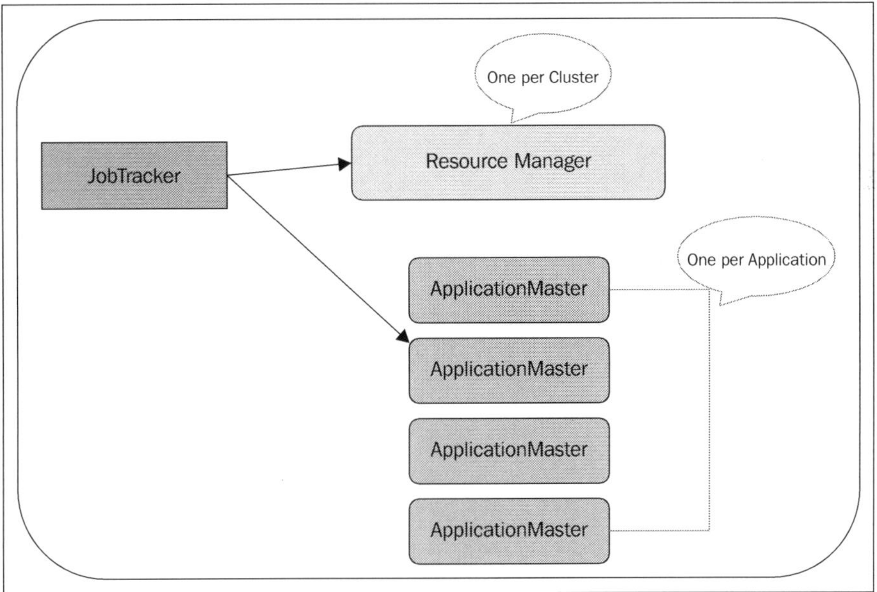

The ResourceManager topology can be seen as follows:

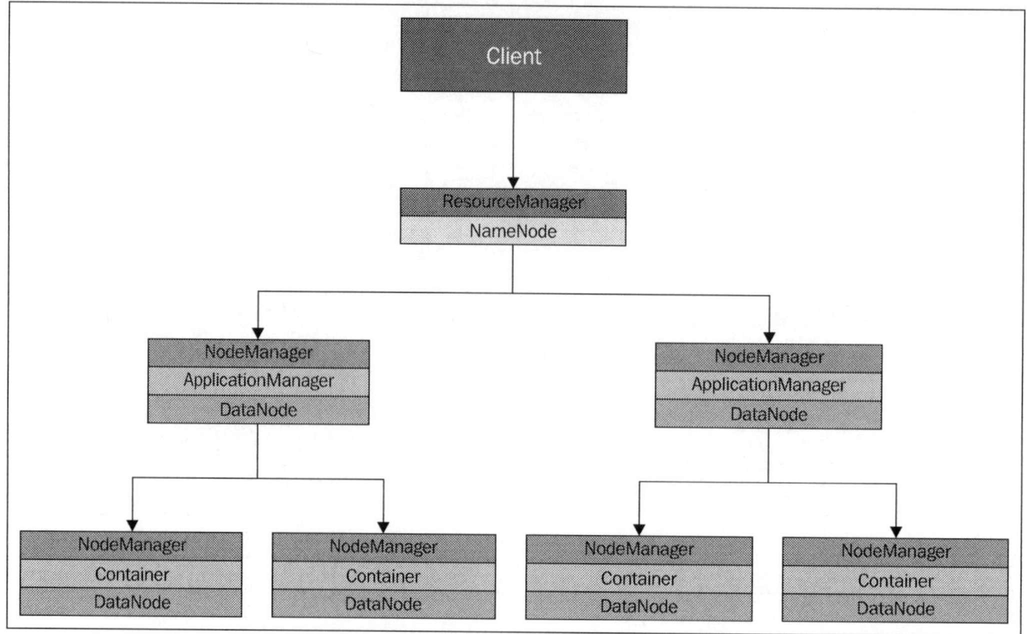

Old and new MapReduce APIs

The new API (which is also known as **Context Objects**) was primarily designed to make the API easier to evolve in the future and is type incompatible with the old one.

The new API came into the picture from the 1.x release series. However, it was partially supported in this series. So, the old API is recommended for 1.x series:

Feature\Release	**1.x**	**0.23**
Old MapReduce API	Yes	Deprecated
New MapReduce API	Partial	Yes
MRv1 runtime (Classic)	Yes	No
MRv2 runtime (YARN)	No	Yes

The old and new API can be compared as follows:

Old API	New API
The old API is in the org.apache.hadoop.mapred package and is still present.	The new API is in the org.apache.hadoop.mapreduce package.
The old API used interfaces for Mapper and Reducer.	The new API uses Abstract Classes for Mapper and Reducer.
The old API used the JobConf, OutputCollector, and Reporter object to communicate with the MapReduce system.	The new API uses the context object to communicate with the MapReduce system.
In the old API, job control was done through the JobClient.	In the new API, job control is performed through the Job class.
In the old API, job configuration was done with a JobConf object.	In the new APO, job configuration is done through the Configuration class via some of the helper methods on Job.
In the old API, both the map and reduce outputs are named part-nnnnn.	In the new API, the map outputs are named part-m-nnnnn and the reduce outputs are named part-r-nnnnn.
In the old API, the reduce() method passes values as a java.lang.Iterator.	In the new API, the . method passes values as a java.lang.Iterable.
The old API controls mappers by writing a MapRunnable, but no equivalent exists for reducers.	The new API allows both mappers and reducers to control the execution flow by overriding the run() method.

Backward compatibility of MRv2 APIs

This section discusses the scope and level of backward compatibility supported in Apache Hadoop MapReduce 2.x (MRv2).

Binary compatibility of org.apache.hadoop.mapred APIs

Binary compatibility here means that the compiled binaries should be able to run without any modification on the new framework.

For those Hadoop 1.x users who use the org.apache.hadoop.mapred APIs, they can simply run their MapReduce jobs on YARN just by pointing them to their Apache Hadoop 2.x cluster via the configuration settings.

They will not need any recompilation. All they will need to do is point their application to the YARN installation and point `HADOOP_CONF_DIR` to the corresponding configuration directory. The `yarn-site.xml` (configuration for YARN) and `mapred-site.xml` files (configuration for MapReduce apps) are present in the conf directory.

Also, `mapred.job.tracker` in `mapred-site.xml` is no longer necessary in Apache Hadoop 2.x. Instead, the following property needs to be added in the `mapred-site.xml` file to make MRv1 applications run on top of YARN:

```
<property>
        <name>mapreduce.framework.name</name>
        <value>yarn</value>
</property>
```

Source compatibility of org.apache.hadoop.mapred APIs

Source incompatibility means that some code changes are required for compilation. Source incompatibility is orthogonal to binary compatibility.

Binaries for an application that is binary compatible but not source compatible will continue to run fine on the new framework. However, code changes are required to regenerate these binaries.

Apache Hadoop 2.x does not ensure complete binary compatibility with the applications that use `org.apache.hadoop.mapreduce` APIs, as these APIs have evolved a lot since MRv1. However, it ensures source compatibility for `org.apache.hadoop.mapreduce` APIs that break binary compatibility. In other words, you should recompile the applications that use MapReduce APIs against MRv2 JARs.

Existing applications that use MapReduce APIs are source compatible and can run on YARN with no changes, recompilation, and/or minor updates.

If an MRv1 MapReduce-based application fails to run on YARN, you are requested to investigate its source code and check whether MapReduce APIs are referred to or not. If they are referred to, you have to recompile the application against the MRv2 JARs that are shipped with Hadoop 2.

Practical examples of MRv1 and MRv2

We will now present a MapReduce example using both the old and new MapReduce APIs.

We will now write a MapReduce program in Java that finds all the **anagrams** (a word, phrase, or name formed by rearranging the letters of another, such as cinema, formed from iceman) presents them in an input file, and finally prints all the anagrams in the output file.

Here is the `AnagramMapperOldAPI.java` class that uses the old MapReduce API:

```
import java.io.IOException;
import java.util.Arrays;

import org.apache.hadoop.io.Text;
import org.apache.hadoop.mapred.MapReduceBase;
import org.apache.hadoop.mapred.Mapper;
import org.apache.hadoop.mapred.OutputCollector;
import org.apache.hadoop.mapred.Reporter;

import java.util.StringTokenizer;


/**
 * The Anagram mapper class gets a word as a line from the HDFS
    input and sorts the
 * letters in the word and writes its back to the output collector
    as
 * Key : sorted word (letters in the word sorted)
 * Value: the word itself as the value.
 * When the reducer runs then we can group anagrams together based
    on the sorted key.
 */
public class AnagramMapperOldAPI extends MapReduceBase implements
    Mapper<Object, Text, Text, Text> {

  private Text sortedText = new Text();
  private Text originalText = new Text();

  @Override
  public void map(Object keyNotUsed, Text value,
```

```
        OutputCollector<Text, Text> output, Reporter reporter)
        throws IOException {

      String line = value.toString().trim().toLowerCase().replace(",",
"");
      System.out.println("LINE:"+line);

      StringTokenizer st = new StringTokenizer(line);

      System.out.println("---- Split by space ------");
      while (st.hasMoreElements()) {
        String word = (String) st.nextElement();

        char[] wordChars = word.toCharArray();
        Arrays.sort(wordChars);
        String sortedWord = new String(wordChars);

        sortedText.set(sortedWord);
        originalText.set(word);

        System.out.println("\torig:" + word + "\tsorted:" +
          sortedWord);

        output.collect(sortedText, originalText);

      }
    }
  }
```

Here is the `AnagramReducerOldAPI.java` class that uses the old MapReduce API:

```
import java.io.IOException;
import java.util.Iterator;
import java.util.StringTokenizer;

import org.apache.hadoop.io.Text;
import org.apache.hadoop.mapred.MapReduceBase;
import org.apache.hadoop.mapred.OutputCollector;
import org.apache.hadoop.mapred.Reducer;
```

```
import org.apache.hadoop.mapred.Reporter;

public class AnagramReducerOldAPI extends MapReduceBase implements
    Reducer<Text, Text, Text, Text> {

  private Text outputKey = new Text();
  private Text outputValue = new Text();

  public void reduce(Text anagramKey, Iterator<Text>
    anagramValues,
      OutputCollector<Text, Text> output, Reporter reporter)
      throws IOException {
    String out = "";

    // Considering words with length > 2
    if (anagramKey.toString().length() > 2) {

      System.out.println("Reducer Key: " + anagramKey);

      while (anagramValues.hasNext()) {
        out = out + anagramValues.next() + "~";
      }

      StringTokenizer outputTokenizer = new StringTokenizer(out,
        "~");
      if (outputTokenizer.countTokens() >= 2) {
        out = out.replace("~", ",");
        outputKey.set(anagramKey.toString() + "  -->    ");
        outputValue.set(out);
        System.out.println("************ Writing reducer output:"
          +anagramKey.toString() + "  -->    " +out);
        output.collect(outputKey, outputValue);
      }
    }
  }
}
```

Finally, to run the MapReduce program, we have the `AnagramJobOldAPI.java` class written using the old MapReduce API:

```
import org.apache.hadoop.fs.Path;
import org.apache.hadoop.io.Text;
import org.apache.hadoop.mapred.FileInputFormat;
import org.apache.hadoop.mapred.FileOutputFormat;
import org.apache.hadoop.mapred.JobClient;
import org.apache.hadoop.mapred.JobConf;

public class AnagramJobOldAPI {

  public static void main(String[] args) throws Exception {
    if (args.length != 2) {
      System.err.println("Usage: Anagram <input path> <output
        path>");
      System.exit(-1);
    }

    JobConf conf = new JobConf(AnagramJobOldAPI.class);
    conf.setJobName("Anagram Job Old API");

    FileInputFormat.addInputPath(conf, new Path(args[0]));
    FileOutputFormat.setOutputPath(conf, new Path(args[1]));

    conf.setMapperClass(AnagramMapperOldAPI.class);
    conf.setReducerClass(AnagramReducerOldAPI.class);

    conf.setOutputKeyClass(Text.class);
    conf.setOutputValueClass(Text.class);

    JobClient.runJob(conf);

  }

}
```

Next, we will write the same Mapper, Reducer, and Job classes using the new MapReduce API.

Here is the `AnagramMapper.java` class that uses the new MapReduce API:

```
import java.io.IOException;
import java.util.Arrays;
import java.util.StringTokenizer;

import org.apache.hadoop.io.Text;
import org.apache.hadoop.mapreduce.Mapper;

public class AnagramMapper extends Mapper<Object, Text, Text,
  Text> {

  private Text sortedText = new Text();
  private Text orginalText = new Text();

  @Override
  public void map(Object key, Text value, Context context)
      throws IOException, InterruptedException {

    String line = value.toString().trim().toLowerCase().replace(",",
"");
    System.out.println("LINE:" + line);

    StringTokenizer st = new StringTokenizer(line);

    System.out.println("---- Split by space ------");
    while (st.hasMoreElements()) {
      String word = (String) st.nextElement();

      char[] wordChars = word.toCharArray();
      Arrays.sort(wordChars);
      String sortedWord = new String(wordChars);

      sortedText.set(sortedWord);
      orginalText.set(word);

      System.out.println("\torig:" + word + "\tsorted:" +
        sortedWord);

      context.write(sortedText, orginalText);
    }
  }
}
```

Here is the `AnagramReducer.java` class that uses the new MapReduce API:

```
import java.io.IOException;
import java.util.StringTokenizer;

import org.apache.hadoop.io.Text;
import org.apache.hadoop.mapreduce.Reducer;

public class AnagramReducer extends Reducer<Text, Text, Text,
  Text> {

  private Text outputKey = new Text();
  private Text outputValue = new Text();

  public void reduce(Text anagramKey, Iterable<Text>
    anagramValues,
      Context context) throws IOException, InterruptedException {
    String out = "";


    if (anagramKey.toString().length() > 2) {

      System.out.println("Reducer Key: " + anagramKey);

      for (Text anagram : anagramValues) {
        out = out + anagram.toString() + "~";
      }

      StringTokenizer outputTokenizer = new StringTokenizer(out,
        "~");
      if (outputTokenizer.countTokens() >= 2) {
        out = out.replace("~", ",");
        outputKey.set(anagramKey.toString()+"   -->     ");
        outputValue.set(out);
        System.out.println("****** Writing reducer output:"
          +anagramKey.toString() + "   -->     " +out);
        context.write(outputKey, outputValue);
      }
    }
  }
}
```

Finally, here is the `AnagramJob.java` class that uses the new MapReduce API:

```
import org.apache.hadoop.fs.Path;
import org.apache.hadoop.io.Text;
import org.apache.hadoop.mapreduce.Job;
import org.apache.hadoop.mapreduce.lib.input.FileInputFormat;
import org.apache.hadoop.mapreduce.lib.output.FileOutputFormat;

public class AnagramJob {

  public static void main(String[] args) throws Exception {
    if (args.length != 2) {
     System.err.println("Usage: Anagram <input path> <output path>");
     System.exit(-1);
    }

    Job job = new Job();
    job.setJarByClass(AnagramJob.class);
    job.setJobName("Anagram Job");

    FileInputFormat.addInputPath(job, new Path(args[0]));
    FileOutputFormat.setOutputPath(job, new Path(args[1]));

    job.setMapperClass(AnagramMapper.class);
    job.setReducerClass(AnagramReducer.class);

    job.setOutputKeyClass(Text.class);
    job.setOutputValueClass(Text.class);

    System.exit(job.waitForCompletion(true) ? 0 : 1);
   }
}
```

Preparing the input file(s)

1. Create a `${Input file_1}` file with the following contents:

   ```
   The Project Gutenberg Etext of Moby Word II by Grady Ward
   hello there  draw ehllo lemons melons solemn
   Also, bluest bluets bustle sublet subtle
   ```

2. Create another file, `${Input file_2}`, with the following contents:

   ```
   Cinema is anagram to iceman
   Second is stop, tops, opts, pots, and spot
   Stool and tools
   Secure and rescue
   ```

3. Copy these files into `${path_to_your_input_dir}`.

Running the job

Run the `AnagramJobOldAPI.java` class and pass the following as command-line args:

`${path_to_your_input_dir}`

`${path_to_your_output_dir_old}`

Now, run the `AnagramJob.java` class and pass the following as command-line args:

`${path_to_your_input_dir}`

`${path_to_your_output_dir_new}`

Result

The final output written to is `${path_to_your_output_dir_old}` and `${path_to_your_output_dir_new}`.

These are the contents that we will see in the output file:

```
aceimn  -->      cinema,iceman,
adn  -->      and,and,and,
adrw  -->      ward,draw,
belstu  -->      subtle,bustle,bluets,bluest,sublet,
ceersu  -->      rescue,secure,
ehllo  -->      hello,ehllo,
elmnos  -->      lemons,melons,solemn,
loost  -->      stool,tools,
opst  -->      pots,tops,stop,spot,opts,
```

Summary

In this chapter, we started with a brief history of Hadoop releases. Next, we covered the basics of Hadoop 1.x and MRv1. We then looked at the core differences between MRv1 and MRv2 and how YARN fits into a Hadoop environment. We also saw how the JobTracker's responsibilities were broken down in Hadoop 2.x.

We also talked about the old and new MapReduce APIs, their origin, differences, and support in YARN. Finally, we concluded the chapter with some practical examples using the old and new MapReduce APIs.

In the next chapter, you will learn about the administration part of YARN.

5

YARN Administration

In this section, we will focus on YARN's administrative part and on the administrator roles and responsibilities of YARN. We will also gain a more detailed insight into the administration configuration settings and parameters, application container monitoring, and optimized resource allocations, as well as scheduling and multitenancy application support in YARN. We'll also cover the basic administration tools and configuration options of YARN.

The following topics will be covered in this chapter:

- YARN container allocation and configurations
- Scheduling policies
- YARN multitenancy application support
- YARN administration and tools

Container allocation

At a very fundamental level, the container is the group of physical resources such as memory, disk, network, CPU, and so on. There can be one or more containers on a single machine; for example, if a machine has 16 GB of RAM and 8 core processors, then a single container could be 1 CPU core and 2 GB of RAM. This means that there are a total of 8 containers on a single machine, or there could be a single large container with all the occupied resources. So, a container is a physical notation of memory, CPU, network, disk, and so on in the cluster. The container's life cycle is managed by the NodeManager, and the scheduling is done by the ResourceManager. The container allocation can be seen as follows:

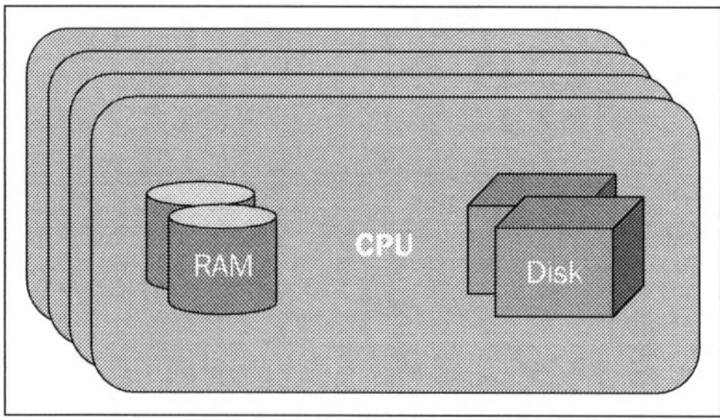

YARN is designed to allocate resource containers to the individual applications in a shared, secure, and multitenant manner. When any job or task is submitted to the YARN framework, the ResourceManager takes care of the resource allocations to the application, depending on scheduling configurations and the application's needs and requirements via the ApplicationMaster. To achieve this goal, the central scheduler maintains the metadata about all the application's resource requirements; this leads to efficient scheduling decisions for all the applications that run into the cluster.

Let's take a look at how container allocation happens in a traditional Hadoop setup. In the traditional Hadoop approach, on each node there is a predefined and fixed number of map slots and a predefined and fixed number of reduce slots. The map and reduce functions are unable to share slots, as they are predefined for specific operations only. This static allocation is not efficient; for example, one cluster has a fixed total of 32 map slots and 32 reduce slots. While running a MapReduce application, it took only 16 map slots and required more than 32 slots for reduce operations. The reducer operation is unable to use the 16 free mapper slots, as they are predefined for mapper functionalities only, so the reduce function has to wait until some reduce slots become free.

To overcome this problem, YARN has container slots. Irrespective of the application, all containers are able to run all applications; for example, if YARN has 64 available containers in the cluster and is running the same MapReduce application, if the mapper function takes only 16 slots and the reducer requires more resource slots, then all other free resources in the cluster are allocated to the reducer operation. This makes the operation more efficient and productive.

Essentially, an application demands the required resources from the ResourceManager to satisfy its needs via the ApplicationMaster. Then, by allocating the requested resources to an application, the ResourceManager responds to the application's ResourceRequest. The ResourceRequest contains the name of the resource that has been requested; priority of the request within the various other ResourceRequests of the same application; resource requirement capabilities, such as RAM, disk, CPU, network, and so on; and the number of resources. Container allocation from the ResourceManager to the application means the successful fulfillment of the specific ResourceRequest.

Container allocation to the application

Now, take a look at the following sequence diagram:

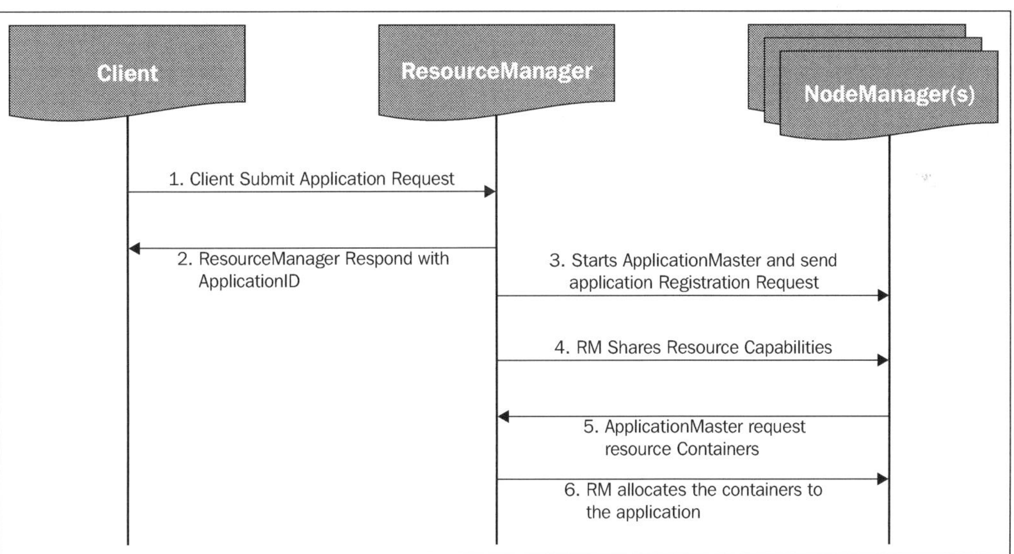

The diagram shows how container allocation is done for applications via the ApplicationMaster. It can be explained as follows:

1. The client submits the application request to the ResourceManager.
2. The ResourceManager registers the application with the ApplicationManager, generates the ApplicationID, and responds to the client with the successfully registered ApplicationID.
3. Then, the ResourceManager starts the client ApplicationMaster in a separate available container. If no container is available, this request has to wait until a suitable container is found and then send the application registration request for application registration.
4. The ResourceManager shares all the minimum and maximum resource capabilities of the cluster with the ApplicationMaster. Then, the ApplicationMaster decides how to efficiently use the available resources to fulfill the application's needs.
5. Depending on the resource capabilities shared by the ResourceManager, the ApplicationMaster requests that the ResourceManager allocates a number of containers on behalf of the application.
6. The ResourceManager responds to the ResourceRequest by the ApplicationMaster as per the scheduling policies and resource availability. Container allocation by the ResourceManager means the successful fulfillment of the ResourceRequest by the ApplicationMaster.

While running the job, the ApplicationMaster sends the heartbeat and job progress information of the application to the ResourceManager. During the runtime of the application, the ApplicationMaster requests for the release or allocation of more containers from the ResourceManager. When the job finishes, the ApplicationMaster sends a container de-allocation request to the ResourceManager and exits itself from running the container.

Container configurations

Here are the some important configurations related to resource containers that are used to control containers.

To control the memory allocation to a container, the administrator needs to set the following three parameters in the `yarn-site.xml` configuration file:

Parameter	Description
`yarn.nodemanager.resource.memory-mb`	This is the amount of memory in MBs that the NodeManager can use for the containers.
`yarn.scheduler.minimum-allocation-mb`	This is the smallest amount of memory in MBs allocated to the container by the ResourceManager. The default value is 1024 MB.
`yarn.scheduler.maximum-allocation-mb`	This is the largest amount of memory in MBs allocated to the container by the ResourceManager. The default value is 8192 MB.

The CPU core allocations to the container are controlled by setting the following properties in the `yarn-site.xml` configuration file:

Parameter	Description
`yarn.scheduler.minimum-allocation-vcores`	This is the minimum number of CPU cores that are allocated to the container.
`yarn.scheduler.maximum-allocation-vcores`	This is the maximum number of CPU cores that are allocated to the container.
`yarn.nodemanager.resource.cpu-vcores`	This is the number of cores that the container can request for the node.

YARN scheduling policies

The YARN architecture has pluggable scheduling policies that depend on the application's requirements and the use case defined for the running application. You can find the YARN scheduling configurations in the `yarn-site.xml` file. Here, you can specify the scheduling system as either FIFO, capacity, or fair scheduling as per the application's needs. You can also find the running application scheduling information in the ResourceManager UI. Many components of the scheduling system are defined briefly there.

As already mentioned, there are three type of scheduling policies that the YARN scheduler follows:

- FIFO scheduler
- Capacity scheduler
- Fair scheduler

The FIFO (First In First Out) scheduler

This is the scheduling policy introduced into the system from Hadoop 1.0. The JobTracker was used to be FIFO scheduling policies. As the name indicates, FIFO means First in First Out, that is, the job submitted first will execute first. The FIFO scheduler policy does not follow any application priorities; this policy might efficiently work for smaller jobs, but while executing larger jobs, FIFO works very inefficiently. So for heavy-loaded clusters, this policy is not recommended.
The FIFO scheduler can be seen as follows:

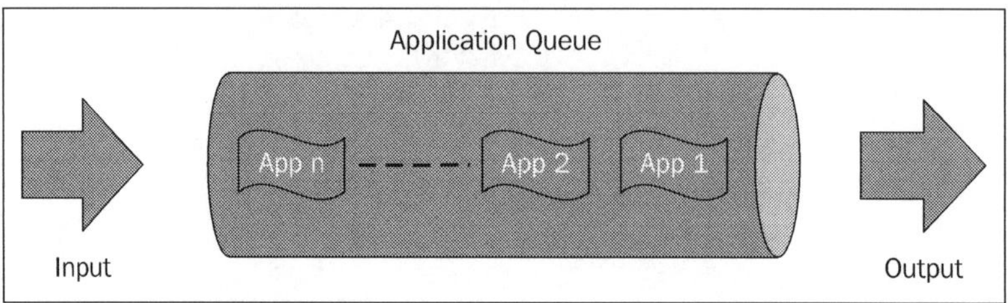

The FIFO (First In First Out) scheduler

Here is the configuration property for the FIFO scheduler. By specifying this in `yarn-site.xml`, you can enable the FIFO scheduling policy in your YARN cluster:

```
<property>
<name>yarn.resourcemanager.scheduler.class</name>
<value>org.apache.hadoop.yarn.server.resourcemanager.scheduler.
  fifo.FifoScheduler </value>
</property>
```

The capacity scheduler

The capacity scheduling policy is one of the very famous pluggable scheduler policies that allows multiple applications or user groups to share the Hadoop cluster resources in a secure way. Nowadays, this scheduling policy runs successfully on many of the largest Hadoop production clusters in an efficient way.

The capacity scheduling policy allows a user or user groups to share cluster resources in such a way that each user or group of users would get assigned a certain capacity of the cluster for sure. To enable this policy, the cluster administrator configures one or more queues with some precalculated shares of the total cluster resource capacity; this assignment guarantees the minimum resource capacity allocation to each queue. The administrator can also configure the maximum and minimum constraints on the use of cluster resources (capacity) on each queue. Each queue has its own **Access Control List** (**ACL**) policies that can manage which user has permission to submit the applications on which queues. ACLs also manage the read and modify permissions at the queue level so that users cannot view or modify the applications submitted by other users.

Capacity scheduler configurations

Capacity scheduler configurations come with Hadoop YARN by default. Sometimes, it is necessary to configure the policy in YARN configuration files. Here are the configuration properties that need to be specified in `yarn-site.xml` to enable the capacity scheduler policy:

```
<property>
<name>yarn.resourcemanager.scheduler.class</name>
<value>org.apache.hadoop.yarn.server.resourcemanager.scheduler.
  capacity.CapacityScheduler </value>
</property>
```

The capacity scheduler, by default, comes with its own configuration file named `$HADOOP_CONF_DIR/capacity-scheduler.xml`; this should be present in the classpath so that the ResourceManager is able to locate it and load the properties for this accordingly.

The fair scheduler

The fair scheduler is one of the most famous pluggable schedulers for large clusters. It enables memory-intensive applications to share cluster resources in a very efficient way. Fair scheduling is a policy that enables the allocation of resources to applications in a way that all applications get, on average, an equal share of the cluster resources over a given period.

In a fair scheduling policy, if one application is running on the cluster, it might request all cluster resources for its execution, if needed. If other applications are submitted, the policy can distribute the free resources among the applications in such a way that each application gets a fairly equal share of cluster resources. A fair scheduler also follows a preemption where the ResourceManager might request the resource containers back from the ApplicationMaster, depending on the job configurations. It might be a healthy or an unhealthy preemption.

In this scheduling model, every application is part of a queue, so resources are assigned to the queue. By default, each user shares the queue called 'Default Queue'. A fair scheduler supports many features at the queue level, such as assigning weight to the queue. A heavyweight queue would get a higher number of resources than lightweight queues, minimum and maximum shares that queue would get FIFO policy within the queue.

While submitting the application, users might specify the name of the queue the application wants to use resources from. For example, if the application requires a higher number of resources, it can specify the heavyweight queue so that it can get all the required resources that are available there.

The advantage of using the fair scheduling policy is that every queue would get a minimum share of the cluster resources. It is very important to note that when a queue contains applications that are waiting for the resources, they would get the minimum resource share. On the other hand, if the queues resources are more than enough for the application, then the excess amount would be distributed equally among the running applications.

Fair scheduler configurations

To enable the fair scheduling policy in your YARN cluster, you need to specify the following property in the `yarn-site.xml` file:

```
<property>
<name>yarn.resourcemanager.scheduler.class</name>
<value>org.apache.hadoop.yarn.server.resourcemanager.
  scheduler.fair.FairScheduler </value>
</property>
```

The fair scheduler also has a specific configuration file for a more detailed configuration setup; you will find it at `$HADOOP_CONF_DIR/fair-scheduler.xml`.

YARN multitenancy application support

YARN comes with built-in multitenancy support. Now, let's have a look at what multitenancy means. Consider a society that has multiple apartments in it, so there are different types of family living in different apartments with security and privacy, but they all share the society's common areas, such as the society gate, garden, play area, and other amenities. Their apartments also share common walls. The same concept is followed in YARN: the that run running into the cluster share the cluster resources in a multitenant way. They share cluster processing capacity, cluster storage capacity, data access securities, and so on. Multitenancy is achieved in the cluster by differentiating applications into multiple business units, for example, different queues and users for different types of applications.

Security and privacy can be achieved by configuring Linux and HDFS permissions to separate files and directories to create tenant boundaries. This can be achieved by integrating with LDAP or Active Directory. Security is used to enforce the tenant application boundaries, and this can be integrated with the Kerberos security model.

The following diagram will explain how an application runs in the YARN cluster in a multitenant way:

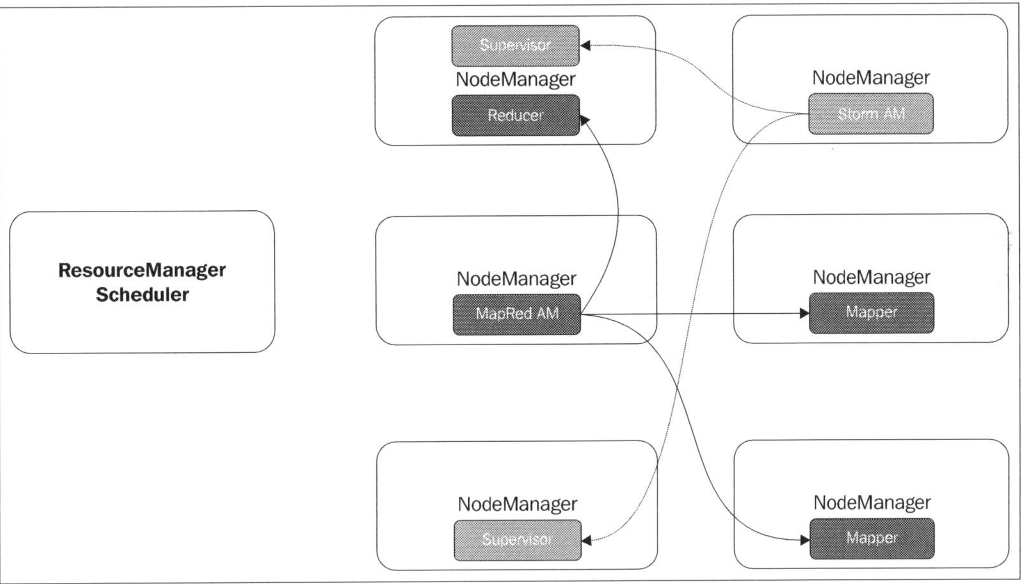

In the preceding YARN cluster, you can see that two jobs are running: one is Storm, and the other is the MapReduce job. They are sharing the cluster scheduler, cluster processing capacity, HDFS storage, and cluster security. We can also see the two applications are running on a single YARN cluster. The MapReduce and Storm jobs are running over YARN and sharing the common cluster infrastructure, CPU, RAM, and so on. The Storm ApplicationMaster, Storm Supervisor, MapRed ApplicationMaster, Mappers, and Reducers are running over the YARN cluster in a multitenant way by sharing cluster resources.

Administration of YARN

Now, we will take a look at some YARN basic administration configurations, basically from Hadoop 2.0. YARN was introduced and made changes in Hadoop configuration files. Hadoop and YARN have the following basic configuration files:

- `core-default.xml`: This file contains properties related to the system.
- `hdfs-default.xml`: This file contains HDFS-related configurations.
- `mapred-default.xml`: This configuration file contains properties related to the YARN MapReduce framework.
- `yarn-default.xml`: This file contains YARN-related properties.

You will find all these properties listed on the Apache website (`http://hadoop.apache.org/docs/current/`) in the configuration section, with detailed information on each property and its default and possible values.

Administrative tools

YARN has several administrative tools by default; you can find them using the `rmadmin` command. Here is a more detailed explanation of the ResourceManager admin command:

```
$ yarn rmadmin -help
```

The `rmadmin` command is the command to execute MapReduce administrative commands. The full syntax is:

```
hadoop rmadmin [-refreshQueues] [-refreshNodes]
[-refreshSuperUserGroupsConfiguration] [-refreshUserToGroupsMappings]
[-refreshAdminAcls] [-refreshServiceAcl] [-getGroup [username]] [-help
[cmd]]
```

The preceding command contains the following fields:

- `-refreshQueues`: Reloads the queues' acls, states, and scheduler-specific properties. The ResourceManager will reload the `mapred-queues` configuration file.
- `-refreshNodes`: Refreshes the host's information at the ResourceManager.
- `-refreshUserToGroupsMappings`: Refreshes user-to-groups mappings.
- `-refreshSuperUserGroupsConfiguration`: Refreshes superuser proxy groups mappings.
- `-refreshAdminAcls`: Refreshes acls for the administration of the ResourceManager.
- `-refreshServiceAcl`: Reloads the service-level authorization policy file. ResourceManager will reload the authorization policy file.
- `-getGroups [username]`: Get the groups that the given user belongs to.
- `-help [cmd]`: Displays help for the given command, or all commands if none is specified.

The generic options supported are as follows:

- `-conf <configuration file>`: This will specify an application configuration file.
- `-D <property=value>`: This will use the value for the given property.
- `-fs <local|namenode:port>`: This will specify a NameNode.
- `-jt <local|jobtracker:port>`: This will specify a JobTracker.
- `-files <comma separated list of files>`: This will specify comma-separated files to be copied to the MapReduce cluster.
- `-libjars <comma separated list of jars>`: This will specify comma-separated JAR files to include in the class path.
- `-archives <comma separated list of archives>`: This will specify comma-separated archives to be unarchived on the compute machines.

The general command line syntax is:

```
bin/hadoop command [genericOptions] [commandOptions]
```

Adding and removing nodes from a YARN cluster

A YARN cluster is horizontally scalable; you can add or remove worker nodes in or from the cluster without stopping it. To add a new node, all the software and configurations must be done over the new node.

The following property is used to add a new node to the cluster:

```
yarn.resourcemanager.nodes.include-path
```

For removing the node from the cluster, the following property is used:

```
yarn.resourcemanager.exclude-path
```

The preceding two properties take values as a local file that contains the list of nodes that need to be added or removed from the cluster. This file contains either the hostnames or the IPs of the worker nodes separated by a new line, tab, or space.

After adding or removing the node, the YARN cluster does not require a restart. It just needs to refresh the list of worker nodes so that the ResourceManager gets informed about the newly added or removed nodes:

```
$ yarn rmadmin -refreshNodes
```

Administrating YARN jobs

The most important YARN admin task is administrating the running of YARN jobs. You can manage YARN jobs using the `yarn application` CLI command.

Using the `yarn application` command, the administrator can kill a job, list all jobs, and find out the status of a job. MapReduce jobs can be controlled by the `mapred job` command.

Here is the usage of the `yarn application` command:

```
usage: application
-appTypes <Comma-separated list of application types>   Works with--
list to filter applications based on their type.
-help Displays help for all commands.
-kill <Application ID> Kills the application.
-list Lists applications from the RM. Supports optional use of -
appTypes to filter
       applications based on application type.
-status <Application ID> Prints the status of the application.
```

MapReduce job configurations

As MapReduce jobs are now running on YARN containers instead of traditional MapReduce slots, it's necessary to configure MapReduce properties into `mapred-site.xml`. Here are some properties of MapReduce jobs that could be configured to run MapReduce jobs on YARN containers:

Properties	Description
`mapred.child.java.opts`	This property is used to set the Java heap size for child JVMs of maps, for example Xmx4096m.
`mapreduce.map.memory.mb`	This property is used to configure the resource limit for map functions for example, 1536 MB.
`mapreduce.reduce.memory.mb`	This property is used to configure the resource limit for reducer functions, for example 3072 MB.
`mapreduce.reduce.java.opts`	This property is used to set the Java heap size for child JVMs of reducers, for example Xmx4096m.

YARN log management

The log management CLI tool is very useful for YARN application log management. The administrator can use the `logs` CLI command described here:

```
$ yarn logs
Retrieve logs for completed YARN applications.
usage: yarn logs -applicationId <application ID> [OPTIONS]

general options are:
-appOwner <Application Owner>   AppOwner (assumed to be current user
if
                                                     not specified)
-containerId <Container ID>          ContainerId (must be specified if
node
                                                     address is
specified)
-nodeAddress <Node Address>     NodeAddress in the format
nodename:port     (must be specified if container ID is specified)
```

Let's take an example. If you wanted to print all the logs of a specific application, use the following command:

```
$ yarn logs -applicationId <application ID>
```

This command will print all the logs related to the `application_ID` specified in the console's interface.

YARN web user interface

In the YARN web user interface (`http://localhost:8088/cluster`), you can find information on cluster nodes, containers configured on each node, and applications and their status. The YARN web interface is as follows:

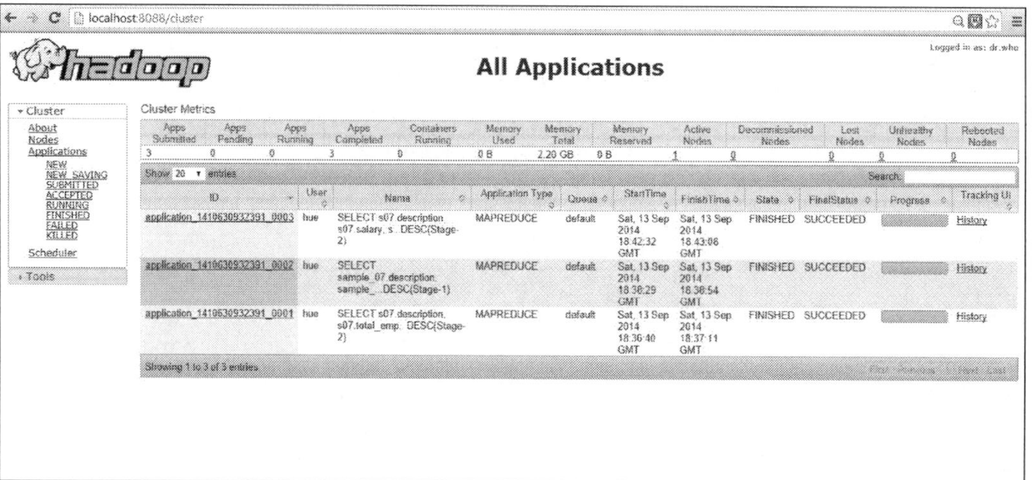

Under the **Scheduler** section, you can see the scheduling information of all the submitted, accepted by the scheduler, running applications, with the total cluster capacity, used and maximum capacity, and resources allocated to the application queue. In the following screenshot, you can see the resources allocated to the default queue:

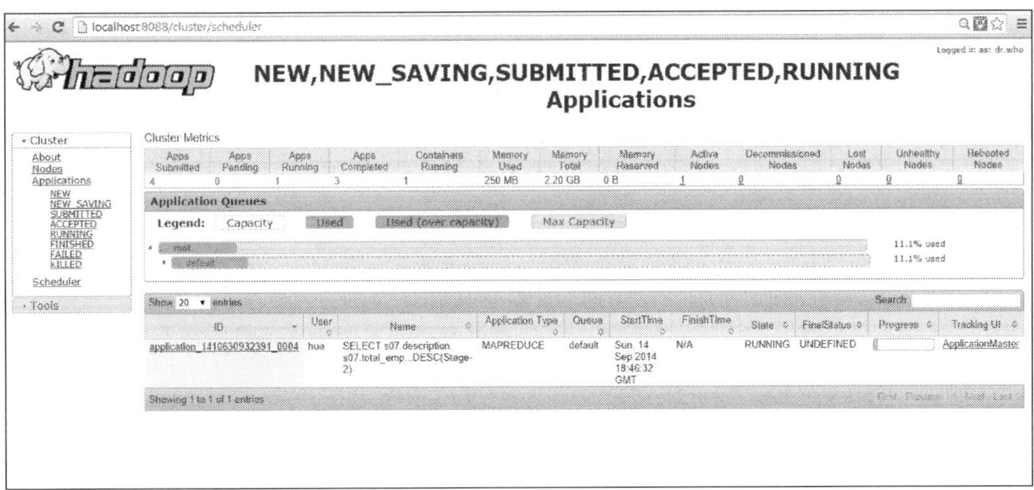

Under the **Tools** section, you can find the YARN configuration file details, scheduling information, container configurations, local logs of the jobs, and a lot of other information on the cluster.

Summary

In this chapter, we covered YARN container allocations and configurations, scheduling policies, and configurations. We also covered multitenancy application support in YARN and some basic YARN administrative tools and settings. In the next chapter, we will cover some useful practical examples about YARN and the ecosystem.

6

Developing and Running a Simple YARN Application

In the previous chapters, we discussed the concepts of the YARN architecture, cluster setup, and administration. Now in this chapter, we will focus more on MapReduce applications with YARN and its ecosystems, with some hands-on examples. You previously learned about when a client submits an application request to the YARN cluster and how YARN registers the application, allocates the required containers for its execution, and monitors the application while it's running. Now, we will see some practical use cases of YARN.

In this chapter, we will discuss:

- Running sample applications on YARN
- Developing YARN examples
- Application monitoring and tracking

Now, let's start by running some of the sample applications that come as a part of the YARN distribution bundle.

Running sample examples on YARN

Running the available sample MapReduce programs is a simple task with YARN. The Hadoop version ships with some basic MapReduce examples. You can find them inside `$HADOOP_HOME/share/Hadoop/mapreduce/Hadoop-mapreduce-examples-<HADOOP_VERSION>.jar`. The location of the file may differ depending on your Hadoop installation folder structure.

Let's include this in the `YARN_EXAMPLES` path:

`$exportYARN_EXAMPLES=$HADOOP_HOME/share/Hadoop/mapreduce`

Now, we have all the sample examples in the YARN_EXAMPLES environmental variable. You can access all the examples using this variable; to list all the available examples, try typing the following command on the console:

```
$ yarn jar $YARN_EXAMPLES/hadoop-mapreduce-examples-2.4.0.2.1.1.0-385.
jar
```

An example program must be given as the first argument.

The valid program names are as follows:

- `aggregatewordcount`: This is an aggregate-based map/reduce program that counts the words in the input files
- `aggregatewordhist`: This is an aggregate-based map/reduce program that computes the histogram of the words in the input files
- `bbp`: This is a map/reduce program that uses Bailey-Borwein-Plouffe to compute the exact digits of Pi
- `dbcount`: This is an example job that counts the page view counts from a database
- `distbbp`: This is a map/reduce program that uses a BBP-type formula to compute the exact bits of Pi
- `grep`: This is a map/reduce program that counts the matches of a regex in the input
- `join`: This is a job that affects a join over sorted, equally-partitioned datasets
- `multifilewc`: This is a job that counts words from several files
- `pentomino`: This is a map/reduce tile that lays a program to find solutions to pentomino problems
- `pi`: This is a map/reduce program that estimates Pi using a quasi-Monte Carlo method

- `randomtextwriter`: This is a map/reduce program that writes 10 GB of random textual data per node
- `randomwriter`: This is a map/reduce program that writes 10 GB of random data per node
- `secondarysort`: This is an example that defines a secondary sort to the reduce
- `sort`: This is a map/reduce program that sorts the data written by the random writer
- `sudoku`: This is a sudoku solver
- `teragen`: This generates data for the terasort
- `terasort`: This runs the terasort
- `teravalidate`: This checks the results of terasort
- `wordcount`: This is a map/reduce program that counts the words in the input files
- `wordmean`: This is a map/reduce program that counts the average length of the words in the input files
- `wordmedian`: This is a map/reduce program that counts the median length of the words in the input files
- `wordstandarddeviation`: This is a map/reduce program that counts the standard deviation of the length of the words in the input files

These were the sample examples that come as part of the YARN distribution by default. Now, let's try running some of the examples to showcase YARN capabilities.

Running a sample Pi example

To run any application on top of YARN, you need to follow this Java command syntax:

```
$ yarn jar <application_jar.jar><arg0><arg1>
```

To run a sample example to calculate the value of PI with 16 maps and 10,000 samples, use the following command:

```
$ yarn jar $YARN_EXAMPLES/hadoop-mapreduce-examples-2.4.0.2.1.1.0-385.jar
PI 16 10000
```

Note that we are using `hadoop-mapreduce-examples-2.4.0.2.1.1.0-385.jar` here. The JAR version may change depending on your installed Hadoop distribution.

Once you hit the preceding command on the console, you will see the logs generated by the application on the console, as shown in the following command. The default logger configuration is displayed on the console. The default mode is INFO, and you may change it by overwriting the default logger settings by updating `hadoop.root.logger=WARN,console in conf/log4j.properties`:

```
Number of Maps  = 16
Samples per Map = 10000
Wrote input for Map #0
Wrote input for Map #1
Wrote input for Map #2
Wrote input for Map #3
Wrote input for Map #4
Wrote input for Map #5
Wrote input for Map #6
Wrote input for Map #7
Wrote input for Map #8
Wrote input for Map #9
Wrote input for Map #10
Wrote input for Map #11
Wrote input for Map #12
Wrote input for Map #13
Wrote input for Map #14
Wrote input for Map #15
Starting Job
11/09/14 21:12:02 INFO mapreduce.Job: map 0% reduce 0%
11/09/14 21:12:09 INFO mapreduce.Job: map 25% reduce 0%
11/09/14 21:12:11 INFO mapreduce.Job: map 56% reduce 0%
11/09/14 21:12:12 INFO mapreduce.Job: map 100% reduce 0%
11/09/14 21:12:12 INFO mapreduce.Job: map 100% reduce 100%
11/09/14 21:12:12 INFO mapreduce.Job: Job job_1381790835497_0003 
completed successfully
11/09/14 21:12:19 INFO mapreduce.Job: Counters: 44
  File System Counters
    FILE: Number of bytes read=358
```

```
    FILE: Number of bytes written=1365080
                FILE: Number of read operations=0
                FILE: Number of large read operations=0
                FILE: Number of write operations=0
                HDFS: Number of bytes read=4214
                HDFS: Number of bytes written=215
                HDFS: Number of read operations=67
                HDFS: Number of large read operations=0
                HDFS: Number of write operations=3
        Job Counters
                Launched map tasks=16
                Launched reduce tasks=1
                Data-local map tasks=14
                Rack-local map tasks=2
                Total time spent by all maps in occupied slots
(ms)=184421
                Total time spent by all reduces in occupied slots
(ms)=8542
        Map-Reduce Framework
                Map input records=16
                Map output records=32
                Map output bytes=288
                Map output materialized bytes=448
                Input split bytes=2326
                Combine input records=0
                Combine output records=0
                Reduce input groups=2
                Reduce shuffle bytes=448
                Reduce input records=32
                Reduce output records=0
                Spilled Records=64
                Shuffled Maps =16
                Failed Shuffles=0
```

```
                Merged Map outputs=16
                GC time elapsed (ms)=195
                CPU time spent (ms)=7740
                Physical memory (bytes) snapshot=6143396896
                Virtual memory (bytes) snapshot=23142254400
                Total committed heap usage (bytes)=43340769024
  Shuffle Errors
                BAD_ID=0
                CONNECTION=0
                IO_ERROR=0
                WRONG_LENGTH=0
                WRONG_MAP=0
                WRONG_REDUCE=0
        File Input Format Counters
                Bytes Read=1848
        File Output Format Counters
                Bytes Written=98
Job Finished in 23.144 seconds
Estimated value of Pi is 3.14127500000000000000
```

You can compare the example that runs over Hadoop 1.x and the one that runs over YARN. You can hardly differentiate by looking at the logs, but you can clearly identify the difference in performance. YARN has backward-compatibility support with MapReduce 1.x, without any code change.

Monitoring YARN applications with web GUI

Now, we will look at the YARN web GUI to monitor the examples. You can monitor the application submission ID, the user who submitted the application, the name of the application, the queue in which the application is submitted, the start time and finish time in the case of finished applications, and the final status of the application, using the ResourceManager UI. The ResourceManager web UI differs from the UI of the Hadoop 1.x versions. The following screenshot shows the information we could get from the YARN web UI (`http://localhost:8088`).

Currently, the following web UI is showing information related to the PI example we ran in the previous section, exploring the YARN web UI:

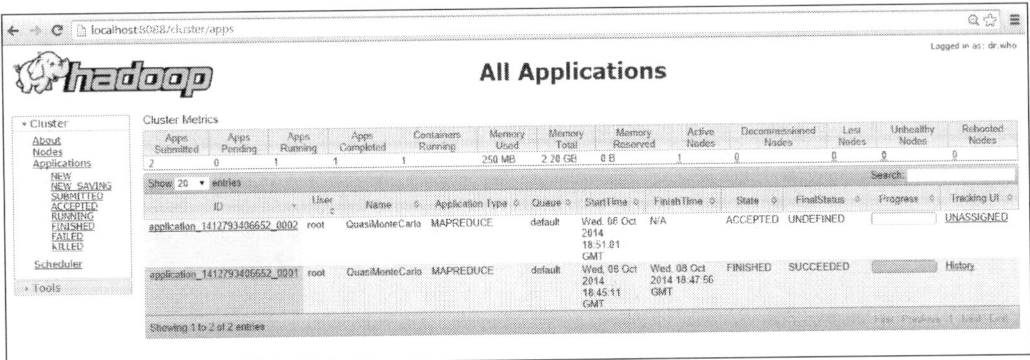

The following screenshot shows the PI example running over the YARN framework and the PI example submitted by the root user into the default queue. An ApplicationMaster is assigned to it, which is currently in the running state. Similarly, you can also monitor all the submitted, accepted and running, finished, and failed jobs' statuses from the ResourceManager web UI.

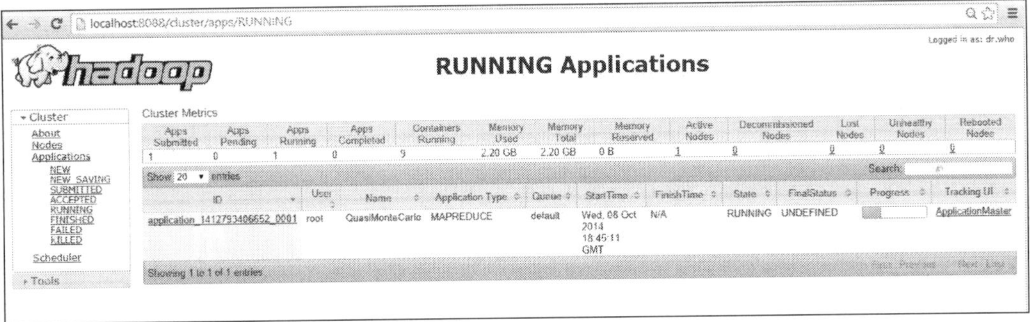

If you drill down further, you can see the application master-level information of the submitted application, such as the total containers allocated to the map and reduce functions and their running status. For example, the following screenshot shows that we already submitted a PI example with 16 mappers. So in the following screenshot, you can see that the total number of containers allocated to the map function is 16, out of which 8 are completed and 8 are in the running state. You can also track the containers allocated to the reduce function and its progress from UI:

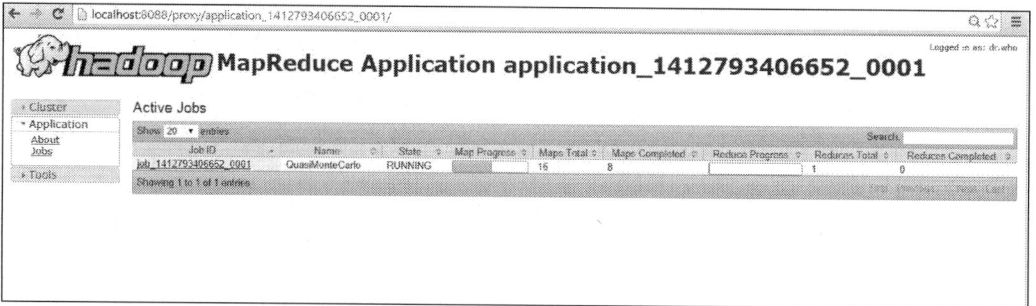

You can see all the information displayed over the console while running the job. The same information will also be displayed on the web UI in a tabular form and in a more sophisticated way:

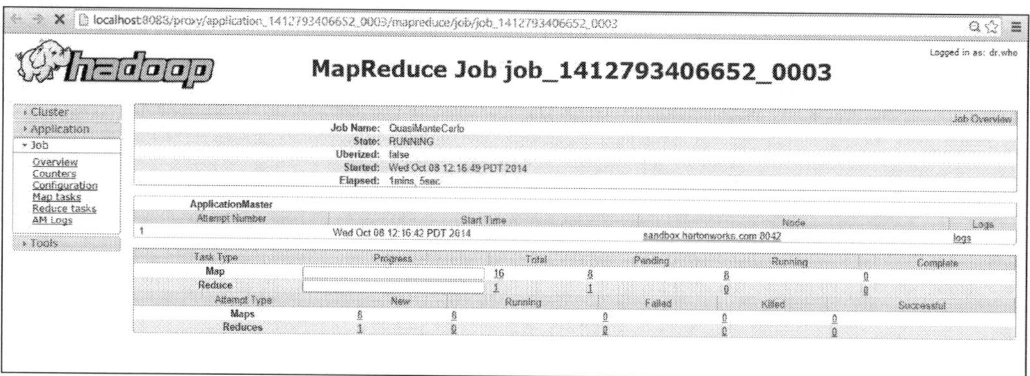

All the mapper and reducer jobs and filesystem counters will be displayed under the counter section of the YARN application web GUI. You can also explore the configurations of the application in the configurations section:

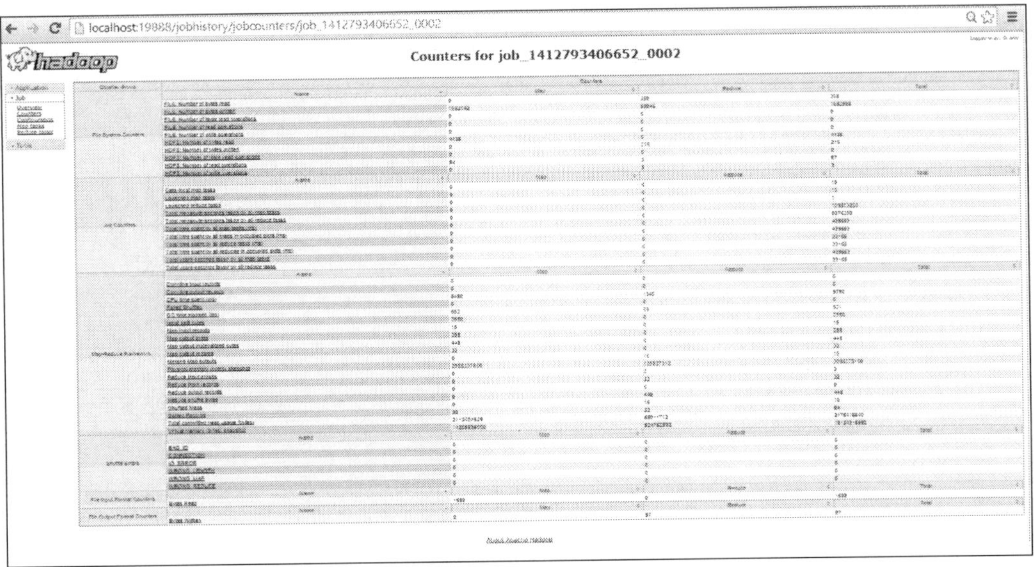

The following screenshot shows the statistics of the finished job, such as the total number of mappers, reducers, start time, finish time, and so on:

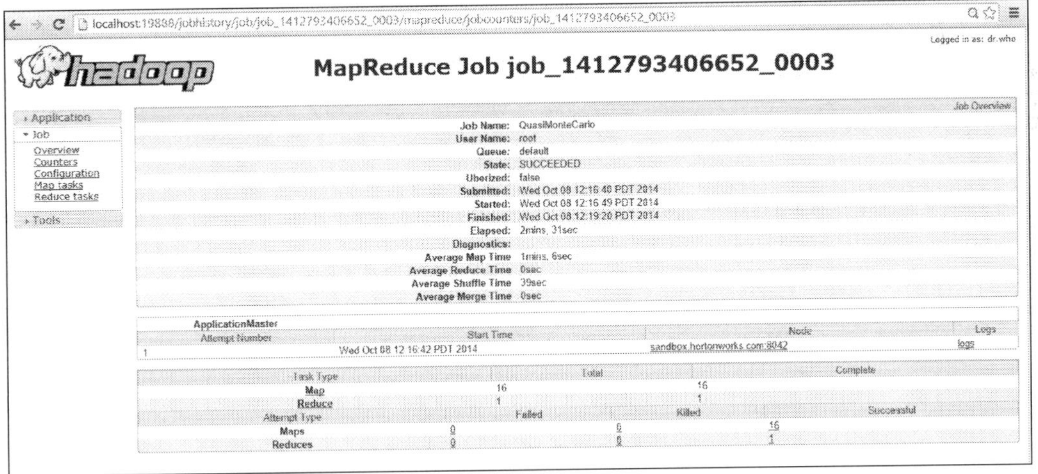

The following screenshot of the YARN web UI gives scheduling information about the YARN cluster, such as the cluster resource capacity and containers allocated to the application or queue:

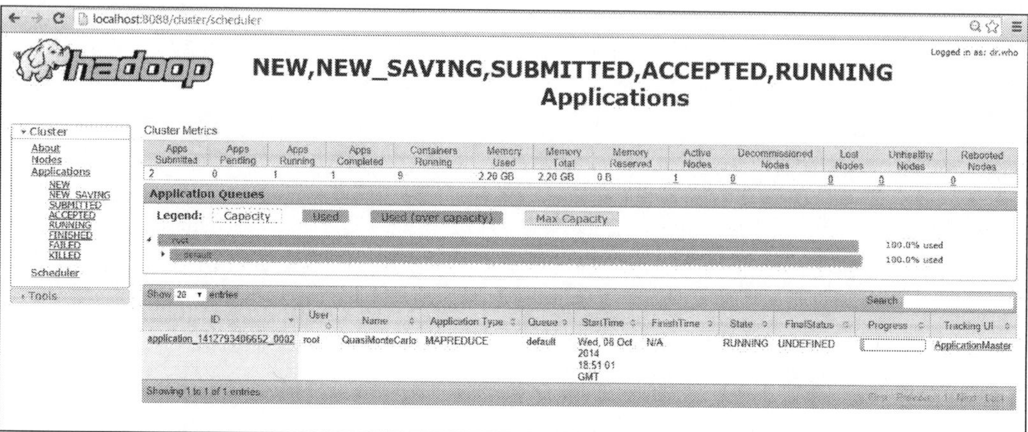

At the end, you will see the job summary page. You may also examine the logs by clicking on the **logs** link provided on the job summary page.

Once a user returns to the main cluster UI, chooses any finished applications, and then selects a job we recently ran, the user will able to see the summary page, as shown in following screenshot:

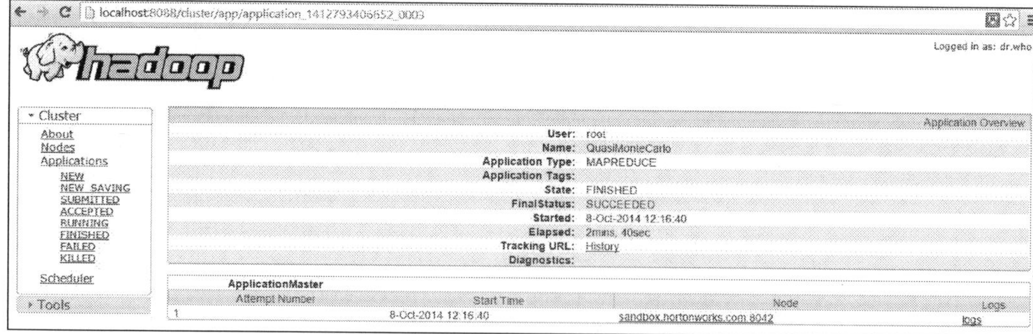

There are a few things to note as we moved through the windows described earlier. First, as YARN manages applications, all input from YARN refers to an application. YARN has no data on the actual application. Data from the MapReduce job is provided by the MapReduce framework. Therefore, there are two clearly different data streams that are combined in the web GUI, YARN applications and MapReduce framework jobs. If the framework does not provide job information, then certain parts of the web GUI will have nothing to display.

A very important fact about YARN jobs is the dynamic nature of the container allocations to the mapper and reducer tasks. These are executed as YARN containers, and their respective number also changes dynamically as per the application's needs and requirements. This feature provides much better cluster utilization due to the dynamic container ("slots" in traditional language) allocations.

YARN's MapReduce support

MapReduce was the only use case on which the previous versions of Hadoop were developed. We know that MapReduce is mainly used for the efficient and effective processing of big data. It is used to process a graph and millions of its nodes and edges. Going forward with technology, to cater for the requirements of data location availability, fault tolerant systems, and application priorities, YARN built support for everything from a simple shell script application to a complex MapReduce application.

For the data location availability, MapReducer's ApplicationMaster has to find out the data block locations and allocations of containers to process these blocks accordingly. Fault tolerant system means the ability to handle failed tasks and act on them accordingly, such as to handle failed map and reduce tasks and rerun them with other containers if needed. Priorities are assigned to each application in the queue; the logic to handle complex intra-application priorities for map and reduce tasks has to be built into the ApplicationMaster. There is no need to start idle reducers before mappers finish enough data processing. Reducers are now under the control of the YARN ApplicationMaster and are not fixed as they had been in Hadoop version 1.

The MapReduce ApplicationMaster

The MapReduce ApplicationMaster service is made up of multiple loosely-coupled services; these services interact with each other via events. Every service gets triggered on an event and produces an output as the event triggers another service; this happens highly concurrently and without synchronization. All service components are registered with the central dispatcher service, and service information is shared between the multiple components via **Application Context** (**AppContext**).

In Hadoop version 1, all the running and submitted jobs are purely dependent on the JobTracker, so the failure of JobTracker results in a loss of all the running and submitted jobs. However, with YARN, the ApplicationMaster is equivalent to the JobTracker. The ApplicationMaster runs and allocates nodes to an application. It may fail, but YARN has the capability to restart the ApplicationMaster a specified number of times and the capability to recover completed tasks. More like JobTracker, the ApplicationMaster keeps the metrics of the jobs currently running. The following settings in the configuration file enable MapReduce recovery in YARN.

To enable the restart of the ApplicationMaster, execute the following steps:

1. Inside `yarn-site.xml`, you can tune the `yarn.resourcemanager.am.max-retries` property. The default is `2`.
2. Inside `mapred-site.xml`, you can directly tune how many times a MapReduce ApplicationMaster should restart with the `mapreduce.am.max-attempts` property. The default is `2`.
3. To enable recovery of completed tasks, look inside the `mapred-site.xml` file. The `yarn.app.mapreduce.am.job.recovery.enable` property enables the recovery of tasks. By default, it is `true`.

Example YARN MapReduce settings

YARN has replaced the fixed slot architecture for mappers and reducers with flexible dynamic container allocation. There are some important parameters to run MapReduce efficiently, and they can be found in `mapred-site.xml` and `yarn-site.xml`. As an example, the following are some settings that have been used to run the MapReduce application on YARN:

Property	Propertyfile	Value
`mapreduce.map.memory.mb`	`mapred-site.xml`	`1536`
`mapreduce.reduce.memory.mb`	`mapred-site.xml`	`2560`
`mapreduce.map.java.opts`	`mapred-site.xml`	`- Xmx1024m`
`mapreduce.reduce.java.opts`	`mapred-site.xml`	`- Xmx2048m`

Property	Propertyfile	Value
yarn.scheduler.minimum-allocation-mb	yarn-site.xml	512
yarn.scheduler.maximum-allocation-mb	yarn-site.xml	4096
yarn.nodemanager.resource.memory-mb	yarn-site.xml	36864
yarn.nodemanager.vmem-pmem-ratio	yarn-site.xml	2.1

YARN configuration allows a container size between 512 MB to 4 GB. If nodes have 36 GB of RAM with a virtual memory of 2.1, each map can have max 3225.6 MB, and each reducer can have 5376 MB of virtual memory. So, the compute node configured for 36 GB of container space can support up to 24 maps and 14 reducers, or any combination of mapper and reducers allowed by the available resources on the node.

YARN's compatibility with MapReduce applications

For a smooth transition from Hadoop v1 to YARN, application backward compatibility has been the major goal of the YARN implementation team to ensure that existing MapReduce applications that were programmed using Hadoop v1 (MRv1) APIs and complied against them can continue to run over YARN, with little enhancement.

YARN ensures full binary compatibility with Hadoop v1 (MRv1) APIs; users who used the `org.apache.hadoop.mapred` APIs provide full compatibility with the YARN framework, without recompilation. You can use your MapReduce JAR file and `bin/hadoop` to submit them directly to YARN.

YARN introduced new API changes for MapReduce applications on top of the YARN framework into `org.apache.hadoop.mapreduce`.

If an application is developed by `org.apache.hadoop.mapreduce` and complied by the Hadoop v1(MRv1) APIs, then unfortunately YARN doesn't provide compatibility with it, as `org.apache.hadoop.mapreduce` APIs have gone through a YARN transition and should be recompiled against Hadoop v2(MRv2) to run over YARN.

Developing YARN applications

To develop a YARN application, you need to keep the YARN architecture in mind. YARN is a platform that allows distributed applications to take full advantage of the resources that YARN has deployed. Currently, resources can be things such as CPU, memory, and data. Many developers who come from a server-side application-development background or from a MapReduce developer background may be accustomed to a certain flow in the development and deployment cycle.

In this section, we'll describe the development life cycle of YARN applications. Also, we'll focus on the key areas of YARN application development, such as how YARN applications can launch containers, how resource allocation has been done for the applications, and many other areas in detail.

The general workflow of the YARN application submission is that the YARNClient communicates with the ResourceManager through the ApplicationClientProtocol to generate a new ApplicationID. It then submits the application to the ResourceManager to run via the ApplicationClientProtocol. As a part of the protocol, the YARNClient has to provide all the required information to the ResourceManager to launch the application's first container, that is, the ApplicationMaster. The YARNClient also needs to provide information details of the dependency JARs/files for the application via command-line arguments. You can also specify the dependency JARs/files in the environment variables.

The following are some interface protocols that the YARN framework will use for intercomponent communication:

- **ApplicationClientProtocol**: This protocol is used by YARN for communication between the YARNClient and ResourceManager to launch a new application, check its status, or to kill the application.
- **ApplicationMasterProtocol**: This protocol is used by the YARN framework to communicate between the ApplicationMaster and ResourceManager. It is used by the ApplicationMaster to register/unregister itself to/from the ResourceManager and also for the resource allocation/deallocation request to the ResourceManager.
- **ContainerManagerProtocol**: This protocol is used for communication between the ApplicationMaster and NodeManager to start and stop containers and their status updates.

The YARN application workflow

Now, take a look at the following sequence diagram that describes the YARN application workflow and also explains how container allocation is done for an application via the ApplicationMaster:

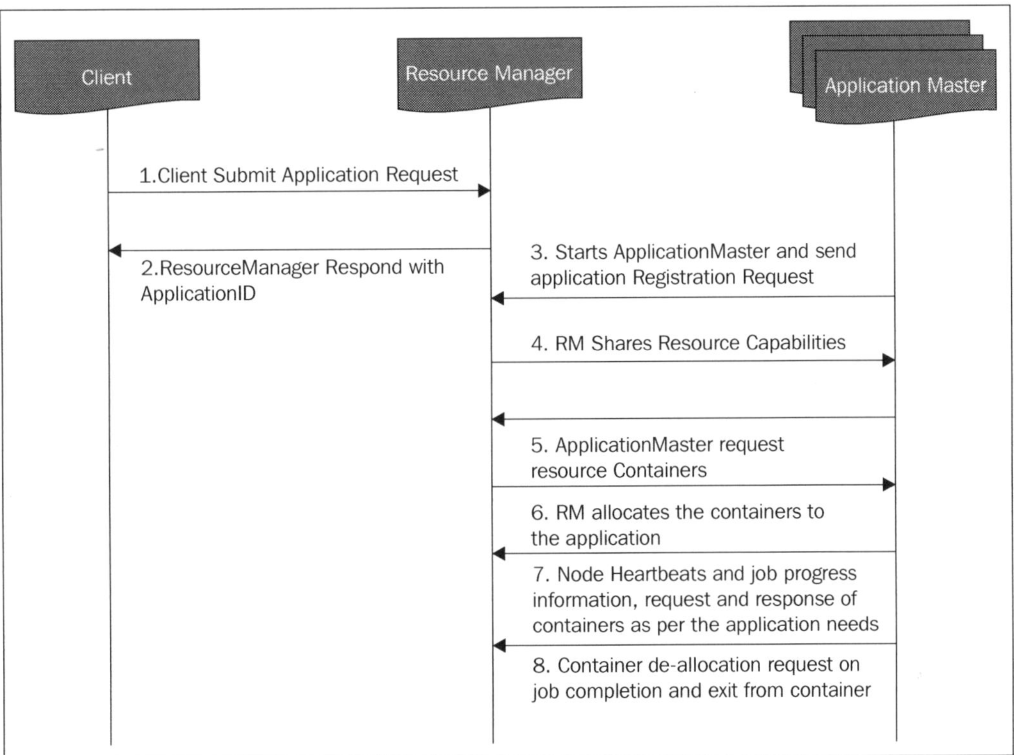

Refer to the preceding diagram for the following details:

- The client submits the application request to the ResourceManager.
- The ResourceManager registers the application with the ApplicationManager, generates the ApplicationID, and responds to the client with the successfully registered ApplicationID.
- Then, the ResourceManager starts the client's ApplicationMaster in a separate available container. If no container is available, then this request has to wait till a suitable container is found, and send the application registration request for application registration.

- The ResourceManager shares all the minimum and maximum resource capabilities of the cluster with the ApplicationMaster. Then, the ApplicationMaster decides how to efficiently use the available resources to fulfill application needs.
- Depending on the resource capabilities shared by the ResourceManager, the ApplicationMaster requests the ResourceManager to allocate the number of containers on behalf of the application.
- The ResourceManager responds to the ResourceRequest by the ApplicationMaster as per the scheduling policies and resource availabilities. Container allocation by the ResourceManager means successful fulfilling of the ResourceRequest by the ApplicationMaster.

While running the job, the ApplicationMaster sends the heartbeat and job progress information of the application to the ResourceManager. During the running time of the application, the ApplicationMaster requests for a release of, or allocates more containers to, the ResourceManager. When the time job finishes, the ApplicationMaster sends a container deallocation request to the ResourceManager, thus exiting itself from the running container.

Writing the YARN client

The YARN client is required to submit the job to the YARN framework. It is a plain Java class, simply having main as entry point function into. The main function of the YARN client is to submit the application to the YARN environment by instantiating the `org.apache.hadoop.yarn.conf.YarnConfiguration` object. The `YarnConfiguration` object depends on finding the `yarn-default.xml` and `yarn-site.xml` files in its class path. All these requirements need to be satisfied to run the YARN client application. The YARN client process is shown in the following image:

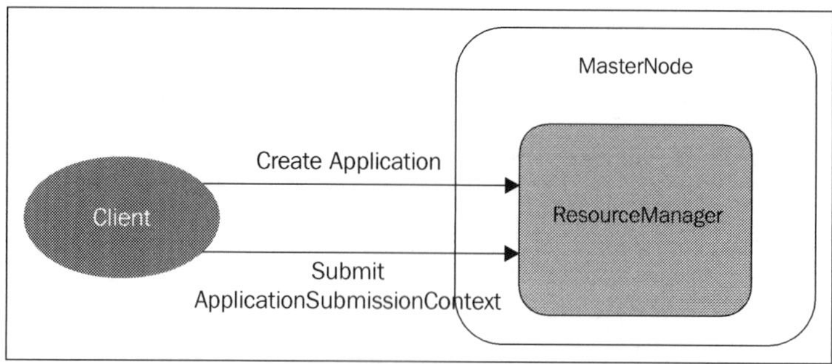

Once a `YarnConfiguration` object is instantiated in your YARN client, we have to create an object of `org.apache.hadoop.client.api.YarnClient` using the `YarnConfiguration` object that has already been instantiated. The newly-instantiated `YarnClient` object will be used to submit the applications to the YARN framework using the following steps:

1. Create an instance of a `YarnClient` object using `YarnConfiguration`.
2. Initialize the YarnClient and the `YarnConfiguration` object.
3. Start a YarnClient.
4. Get the YARN cluster, node, and queue information.
5. Get Access Control List information for the user running the client.
6. Create the client application.
7. Submit the application to the YARN ResourceManager.
8. Get application reports after submitting the application.

Also, the YarnClient will create a context for application submission and for the ApplicationMaster's container launch. The runnable YarnClient will take the command-line arguments from the user who is required to run the job. We'll see the simple code snippet for the YARN application client to get a better idea about it.

The first step of the YARNClient is to connect with the ResourceManager. The following is the code snippet for it:

```
//Declare Application Client Protocol
ApplicationClientProtocol applicationsManager;
//Instamtiate YarnConfiguration
    YarnConfiguration yarnConf = new YarnConfiguration(conf);
//Get the ResourceManager IP address, if not provided use default
    InetSocketAddress rmAddress =
        NetUtils.createSocketAddr(yarnConf.get(
            YarnConfiguration.RM_ADDRESS,
            YarnConfiguration.DEFAULT_RM_ADDRESS));
    LOGGER.info("Connecting to ResourceManager at " + rmAddress);
    configuration appsManagerServerConf = new Configuration(conf);
    appsManagerServerConf.setClass(
        YarnConfiguration.YARN_SECURITY_INFO,
        ClientRMSecurityInfo.class, SecurityInfo.class);
//Initialize ApplicationManager handle
    applicationsManager = ((ApplicationClientProtocol) rpc.getProxy(
        ApplicationClientProtocol.class, rmAddress,
appsManagerServerConf));
```

Once the connection between the YARNClient and ResourceManager is established, the YARNClient needs to request the ApplicationID from theResourceManager:

```
GetNewApplicationRequest newRequest =
    Records.newRecord(GetNewApplicationRequest.class);
GetNewApplicationResponse newResponse =
    applicationsManager.getNewApplication(newRequest);
```

The response from the ApplicationManager is the newly-generated ApplicationID for the application submitted by the YARNClient. You can also get the information related to the minimum and maximum resource capabilities of the cluster (using the GetNewApplicationResponse API). Using this information, developers can set the required resources for the ApplicationMaster container to launch.

The YARNClient needs to set up the following information for the ApplicationSubmissionContext initialization; this information includes all the required information needed by the ResourceManager to launch the ApplicationMaster, as mentioned here:

- Application information, such as ApplicationID generated by the previous step
- Name of the application
- Queue and priority information, such as in which queue the application needs to be submitted and the priorities assigned to the application
- User information, that is, by whom the application is to be submitted
- ContainerLaunchContext, that is, the information needed by the ApplicationMaster to launch local resources (such as JARs, binaries, and files)

It also contains the security-related information (security tokens) and environmental variables (classpath settings) with the command to be executed via the ApplicationMaster:

```
// Create a new launch context for App Master
   ApplicationSubmissionContext appContext =
       Records.newRecord(ApplicationSubmissionContext.class);

// set the ApplicationId
   appContext.setApplicationId(appId);
```

```
    // set the application name
    appContext.setApplicationName(appName);

    // Create a new container launch context for the ApplicationMaster
    ContainerLaunchContext amContainer =
        Records.newRecord(ContainerLaunchContext.class);

    // set the local resources required for the ApplicationMaster
    // local files or archives as needed(for examples jar files)
    Map<String, LocalResource> localResources =
        new HashMap<String, LocalResource>();

    // Copy ApplicationMaster jar to the file system and create
    // local resource to point destination jar path
    FileSystem fs = FileSystem.get(conf);
    Path src = new Path(AppMaster.jar);
    String pathSuffix = appName + "/" + appId.getId() +
    "/AppMaster.jar";
    Path dst = new Path(fs.getHomeDirectory(), pathSuffix);
    // Copy file from src to destionation on HDFS
    fs.copyFromLocal(false,true,src,dst);
    // get HDFS file status from the path where it copied
    FileStatus jarStatus = fs.getFileStatus(dst);
    LocalResource amJarResorce = Records.newRecord(LocalResource.
class);

    // Set the type of resource - file or archive
    // archives are untarred at the destination by the framework
    amJarResorce.setType(LocalResourceType.FILE);
    // Set visibility of the resource
    // Setting to most private option
    amJarResorce.setVisibility(LocalResourceVisibility.APPLICATION);
    // Set the resource to be copied over location
    amJarResorce.setResource(ConverterUtils.getYarnUrlFromPath(dst));
    // Set timestamp and length of file so that the framework
    // can do basic sanity checks for the local resource
    // after it has been copied over to ensure it is the same
    // resource the client intended to use with the application
    amJarResorce.setTimestamp(jarStatus.getModificationTime());

    amJarResorce.setSize(jarStatus.getLen());
    localResources.put("AppMaster.jar",  amJarResorce);
```

```
// Set the local resources into the launch context
amContainer.setLocalResources(localResources);

//set the security tokens as needed
//amContainer.setContainerTokens(containerToken);

// Set up the environment needed for the launch context where the
// ApplicationMaster to be run
Map<String, String> env = new HashMap<String, String>();
// For example, we could setup the classpath needed.
// incase of shell script example, put required resources
env.put(DSConstants.SCLOCATION,HdfsSCLocation);
env.put(DSConstants.SCTIMESTAMP,Long.toString(HdfsSCTimeStamp));
env.put(DSConstants.SCLENGTH,Long.toString(HdfsSCLength));

// Add AppMaster.jar location to the Classpath.
// By default, all the hadoop specific classpaths will already be
// available
// in $CLASSPATH, so we should be careful not to overwrite it.
StringBuilder classPathEnv = new StringBuilder("$CLASSPATH:./*:");
for(String str : conf.get(YarnConfiguration.YARN_APPLICATION_
CLASSPATH).split(",")){
    classPathEnv.append(':');
    classPathEnv.append(str.trim());
}
//add log4j properties into the env variable if required
classPathEnv.append(":./log4j.properties");

env.put("CLASSPATH", classPathEnv);

//set environmental varibales into the container
amContainer.setEnvironment(env);

// set necessary command to be execute the ApplicationMaster
vector<CharSequence> vargs = new Vector<CharSequence>(30);

// set java executable command
vargs.add("${JAVA_HOME}" + "/bin/java");
// set memory Xmx based on AM memory requirements
vargs.add("-Xms" + amMemory + "m");
// set ClassName
vargs.add(amMasterMainClass);
```

```
    // Set parameters for application master
    vargs.add("--container_memory " + String.
valueOf(containerMemory));
    vargs.add("--num_containers " + String.valueOf(numContainers));
    vargs.add("--priority "+String.valueOf(shellCmdPriority));

    if (!shellCommand.isEmpty()) {
       vargs.add("--shell_command " + shellCommand + "");
    }

   if (!shellArgs.isEmpty()) {
       vargs.add("--shell_args " + shellArgs + "");
   }

   for (Map.Entry<String, String> entry : shellEnv.entrySet()) {
        vargs.add("--shell_env " + entry.getKey() + "=" + entry.
getValue());
    }

    if (debugFlag) {
        vargs.add("--debug");
    }

    vargs.add("1>" + ApplicationConstants.LOG_DIR_EXPANSION_VAR + "/
AppMaster.stdout");
    vargs.add("2>" + ApplicationConstants.LOG_DIR_EXPANSION_VAR + "/
AppMaster.stderr");


    // Get final command
    StringBuilder command = new StringBuilder();
    for (CharSequence str : vargs) {
        command.append(str).append(" ");
    }

    List<String> commands = new ArrayList<String>();
    commands.add(command.toString());

    // Set the command array into the container spec

    amContainer.setCommands(commands);

   // For launching an AM container, setting user here is not
```

```
    // needed
    // amContainer.setUser(amUser);

    Resource capability = Records.newRecord(Resource.class);
    // For now only memory is supported, so we set the memory
     capability.setMemory(amMemory);
     amContainer.setResource(capability);

     // Set the container launch content into the
ApplicationSubmissionContext
     appContext.setAMContainerSpec(amContainer);
```

Now the setup process is complete, and our YARNClient is ready to submit the application to the ApplicationManager:

```
     // Create the Applicationrequest to send to the
ApplicationsManager
     SubmitApplicationRequest appRequest =
         Records.newRecord(SubmitApplicationRequest.class);
     appRequest.setApplicationSubmissionContext(appContext);

     // Submit the application to the ApplicationsManager
     // Ignore the response as either a valid response object is
     // returned on
     // success or an exception thrown to denote the failure
     applicationsManager.submitApplication(appRequest);
```

During this process, the ResourceManager will accept all the requests of application submission and allocate containers to the ApplicationMaster to run. The progress of the task submitted by the client can be tracked by communicating with the ResourceManager and requesting an application status report via the ApplicationClientProtocol:

```
GetApplicationReportRequest reportRequest =
          Records.newRecord(GetApplicationReportRequest.class);
      reportRequest.setApplicationId(appId);
      GetApplicationReportResponse reportResponse =
          applicationsManager.getApplicationReport(reportRequest);
      ApplicationReport report =
        reportResponse.getApplicationReport();
```

The response to the report request received from the ResourceManager contains general application information, such as the ApplicationID, the queue information in which the application is running, and information on the user who submitted the application. It also contains the ApplicationMaster details, the host on which the ApplicationMaster is running, and application-tracking information to monitor the progress of the application. The application report also contains the application status information, such as **SUBMITTED**, **RUNNING**, **FINISHED**, and so on.

Also, the client can directly query the ApplicationMaster to get report information via `host:rpc_port` obtained from the ApplicationReport.

Sometimes, the application may be wrongly submitted in another queue or may take longer than usual. In such cases, the client may want to kill the application. The ApplicationClientProtocol supports the forcefully kill operation that can send a kill signal to the ApplicationMaster via the ResourceManager:

```
KillApplicationRequest killRequest =
    Records.newRecord(KillApplicationRequest.class);
killRequest.setApplicationId(appId);
applicationsManager.forceKillApplication(killRequest);
```

Writing the YARN ApplicationMaster

This task is the heart of the whole process. This would be launched by the ResourceManager, and all the necessary information will be provided by the client. As the ApplicationMaster is launched in the first container allocated by the ResourceManager, several parameters are made available by the ResourceManager via environment. These parameters include `containerID` for the ApplicationMaster container, application submission time and details about the NodeManager and the host on which the ApplicationMaster is running. Interactions between the ApplicationMaster and the ResourceManager would require the ApplicationAttemptID. This will be obtained from the ApplicationMaster's ContainerID:

```
Map<String, String> envs = System.getenv();
    String containerIdString =
        envs.get(ApplicationConstants.AM_CONTAINER_ID_ENV);
    if (containerIdString == null) {
      throw new IllegalArgumentException(
          "ContainerId not set in the environment");
    }
    ContainerId containerId = ConverterUtils.toContainerId(containerI
dString);
    ApplicationAttemptId appAttemptID =
      containerId.getApplicationAttemptId();
```

After the successful initialization of the ApplicationMaster, it needs to be registered with the ResourceManager via the ApplicationMasterProtocol. The ApplicationMaster and ResourceManager communicate via the Scheduler interface:

```
    // Connect to the ResourceManager and return handle with RM
    YarnConfiguration yarnConf = new YarnConfiguration(conf);
    InetSocketAddress rmAddress =
        NetUtils.createSocketAddr(yarnConf.get(
            YarnConfiguration.RM_SCHEDULER_ADDRESS,
            YarnConfiguration.DEFAULT_RM_SCHEDULER_ADDRESS));
    LOG.info("Connecting to ResourceManager at " + rmAddress);
    ApplicationMasterProtocol resourceManager =
        (ApplicationMasterProtocol) rpc.getProxy(ApplicationMasterProt
ocol.class, rmAddress, conf);

    // Register the Application Master to the Resource Manager
    // Set the required info into the registration request:
    // ApplicationAttemptId,
    // host on which the app master is running
    // rpc port on which the app master accepts requests from the
client
    // tracking url for the client to track app master progress
    RegisterApplicationMasterRequest appMasterRequest =
      Records.newRecord(RegisterApplicationMasterRequest.class);
    appMasterRequest.setApplicationAttemptId(appAttemptID);
    appMasterRequest.setHost(appMasterHostname);
    appMasterRequest.setRpcPort(appMasterRpcPort);
    appMasterRequest.setTrackingUrl(appMasterTrackingUrl);

    RegisterApplicationMasterResponse response =
      resourceManager.registerApplicationMaster(appMasterRequest);
```

The ApplicationMaster sends status to the ResourceManager via heartbeat signals, and the timeout expiry intervals at the ResourceManager are defined by configuration settings in the YarnConfiguration. The ApplicationMasterProtocol communicates with the ResourceManager to send heartbeats and application progress information.

Depending on application requirements, the ApplicationMaster can request from the ResourceManager the number of container resources to be allocated. For this request, the ApplicationMaster will use the ResourceRequest API to define container specifications. The ResourceRequest will contain the hostname if the containers need to be hosted on specific hosts, or the * wildcard character which implies that any host can fulfill the resource capabilities, such as the memory to be allocated to the container. It will also contain priorities, to set containers that can be allocated to specific tasks on higher priority. For example, in map-reduce tasks, higher priority for a container is allocated to the map task and lower priority for the containers is allocated to the reduce task:

```
// Resource Request
    ResourceRequest request = Records.newRecord(ResourceRequest.
class);

    // setup requirements for hosts
    // whether a particular rack/host is expected
    // Refer to apis under org.apache.hadoop.net for more details
         on
    // using * as any host will do
    request.setHostName("*");

    // set number of containers
    request.setNumContainers(numContainers);

    // set the priority for the request
    Priority pri = Records.newRecord(Priority.class);
    pri.setPriority(requestPriority);
    request.setPriority(pri);

    // Set up resource type requirements
    // For now, only memory is supported so we set memory
         requirements
    Resource capability = Records.newRecord(Resource.class);
    capability.setMemory(containerMemory);
    request.setCapability(capability);
```

After defining the container requests, the ApplicationMaster has to build an allocation request for the ResourceManager. The AllocationRequest consists of the requested containers, containers to be released, the ResponseID (the ID of the response that would be sent back from the allocate call) and progress update information:

```
List<ResourceRequest> requestedContainers;
List<ContainerId> releasedContainers
AllocateRequest req = Records.newRecord(AllocateRequest.class);

// The response id set in the request will be sent back in
// the response so that the ApplicationMaster can
// match it to its original ask and act appropriately.
req.setResponseId(rmRequestID);

// Set ApplicationAttemptId
req.setApplicationAttemptId(appAttemptID);

// Add the list of containers being asked by the AM
req.addAllAsks(requestedContainers);

//ApplicationMaster can request ResourceManager to
    deallocation
// of the container if no longer requires.
 req.addAllReleases(releasedContainers);

// ApplicationMaster can track its progress by setting progess
req.setProgress(currentProgress);

AllocateResponse allocateResponse =
  resourceManager.allocate(req);
```

The response to the container allocation request from the ApplicationMaster to the ResourceManager contains the information on the containers allocated to the ApplicationMaster, the number of hosts available in the cluster, and many more such details.

Containers are not immediately assigned to the ApplicationMaster by the ResourceManager. However, when the container request is sent to the ResourceManager, the ApplicationMaster will eventually get the containers based on cluster-capacity, priorities and cluster-scheduling policy:

```
    // Retrieve list of allocated containers from the response
     List<Container> allocatedContainers =
       allocateResponse.getAllocatedContainers();
     for (Container allocatedContainer : allocatedContainers) {
       LOG.info("Launching shell command on a new container."
           + ", containerId=" + allocatedContainer.getId()
           + ", containerNode=" + allocatedContainer.getNodeId().
getHost()
           + ":" + allocatedContainer.getNodeId().getPort()
           + ", containerNodeURI=" + allocatedContainer.
getNodeHttpAddress()
           + ", containerState" + allocatedContainer.getState()
           + ", containerResourceMemory"
           + allocatedContainer.getResource().getMemory());

       LaunchContainerRunnable runnableLaunchContainer =
           new LaunchContainerRunnable(allocatedContainer);
       Thread launchThread = new Thread(runnableLaunchContainer);
       launchThreads.add(launchThread);
       launchThread.start();
     }

     // Check what the current available resources in the cluster
     Resource availableResources =
       allocateResponse.getAvailableResources();
      LOG.info("Current available resources in the cluster " +
         availableResources);

     // Based on this information, an ApplicationMaster can make
     // appropriate decisions

     // Check the completed containers
     List<ContainerStatus> completedContainers =
         allocateResponse.getCompletedContainersStatuses();
```

```
    for (ContainerStatus containerStatus : completedContainers) {
      LOG.info("Got container status for containerID= "
          + containerStatus.getContainerId()
          + ", state=" + containerStatus.getState()
          + ", exitStatus=" + containerStatus.getExitStatus()
          + ", diagnostics=" + containerStatus.getDiagnostics());

      int exitStatus = containerStatus.getExitStatus();
      if (0 != exitStatus) {
        // container failed
        if (-100 != exitStatus) {
          // application job on container returned a non-zero exit
           // code counts as completed
          numCompletedContainers.incrementAndGet();
          numFailedContainers.incrementAndGet();
        }
        else {
          // something else bad happened
          // app job did not complete for some reason
          // we should re-try as the container was lost for some
           // reason
          numRequestedContainers.decrementAndGet();
          // we do not need to release the container as that has
           // already been done by the
               ResourceManager/NodeManager.
        }
        }
        else {
          // nothing to do
          // container completed successfully
          numCompletedContainers.incrementAndGet();
           LOG.info("Container completed successfully."+ ",
                containerId=" + containerStatus.getContainerId());
         }
      }
    }
```

After container allocation is successfully performed for the ApplicationMaster, it has to set up the ContainerLaunchContext for the tasks on which it will run. Once the ContainerLaunchContext is set, the ApplicationMaster can request the ContainerManager to start the allocated container:

```
    //Assuming an allocated Container obtained from
        AllocateResponse
    // and has been already initialization of container is done
    Container container;
    LOG.debug("Connecting to ContainerManager for containerid=" +
      container.getId());
    // Connect to ContainerManager on the allocated container
    String cmIpPortStr = container.getNodeId().getHost() + ":"
        + container.getNodeId().getPort();
    InetSocketAddress cmAddress =
      NetUtils.createSocketAddr(cmIpPortStr);
    LOG.info("Connecting to ContainerManager at " + cmIpPortStr);
    ContainerManager cm = ((ContainerManager) rpc.
getProxy(ContainerManager.class, cmAddress, conf));

    // Now we setup a ContainerLaunchContext
 LOG.info("Setting up container launch container for containerid=" +
container.getId());
    ContainerLaunchContext ctx =
        Records.newRecord(ContainerLaunchContext.class);

    ctx.setContainerId(container.getId());
    ctx.setResource(container.getResource());

    try {
      ctx.setUser(UserGroupInformation.getCurrentUser().
        getShortUserName());
    } catch (IOException e) {
      LOG.info(
          "Getting current user failed when trying to launch the
            container", + e.getMessage());
    }

    // Set the environment
    Map<String, String> unixEnv;
```

```
// Setup the required env.
// Please note that the launched container does not inherit
// the environment of the ApplicationMaster so all the
// necessary environment settings will need to be re-setup
// for this allocated container.
ctx.setEnvironment(unixEnv);

// Set the local resources
Map<String, LocalResource> localResources =
    new HashMap<String, LocalResource>();
// Again, the local resources from the ApplicationMaster is
     not copied over
// by default to the allocated container. Thus, it is the
     responsibility
      // of the ApplicationMaster to setup all the necessary
           local resources
      // needed by the job that will be executed on the
           allocated container.

// Assume that we are executing a shell script on the
     allocated container
// and the shell script's location in the filesystem is known to
us.
Path shellScriptPath;
LocalResource shellRsrc =
  Records.newRecord(LocalResource.class);
shellRsrc.setType(LocalResourceType.FILE);
shellRsrc.setVisibility(LocalResourceVisibility.APPLICATION);
shellRsrc.setResource(
    ConverterUtils.getYarnUrlFromURI(new
      URI(shellScriptPath)));
shellRsrc.setTimestamp(shellScriptPathTimestamp);
shellRsrc.setSize(shellScriptPathLen);
localResources.put("MyExecShell.sh", shellRsrc);

ctx.setLocalResources(localResources);

// Set the necessary command to execute on the allocated
     container
String command = "/bin/sh ./MyExecShell.sh"
    + " 1>" + ApplicationConstants.LOG_DIR_EXPANSION_VAR +
      "/stdout"
```

```
        + " 2>" + ApplicationConstants.LOG_DIR_EXPANSION_VAR +
          "/stderr";

    List<String> commands = new ArrayList<String>();
    commands.add(command);
    ctx.setCommands(commands);

    // Send the start request to the ContainerManager
    StartContainerRequest startReq = Records.
newRecord(StartContainerRequest.class);
    startReq.setContainerLaunchContext(ctx);

    try{
       cm.startContainer(startReq);
    }catch(YarnRemoteException e){
        LOG.info("Start container failed for :" + ", containerId="
          + container.getId());
         e.printStackTrace();
    }
```

The ApplicationMaster will get the application status information via the ApplicationMasterProtocol. Also, it may monitor by querying the ContainerManager for the application status:

```
    GetContainerStatusRequest statusReq =
        Records.newRecord(GetContainerStatusRequest.class);
    statusReq.setContainerId(container.getId());
    GetContainerStatusResponse statusResp;
     try{
         statucResp = cm.getContainerStatus(statusReq);
    LOG.info("Container Status"
        + ", id=" + container.getId()
        + ", status=" + statusResp.getStatus());
   }catch(YarnRemoteException e){
        e.printStackTrace();
   }
```

This code snippet explains how to write the YARNClient and ApplicationMaster in general. Actually, the ApplicationMaster is the application-specific entity; each application or framework that wants to run over YARN has a different ApplicationMaster, but the flow is the same. For more details on the YARNClient and ApplicationMaster for different frameworks, visit the Apache Foundation website.

Responsibilities of the ApplicationMaster

The ApplicationMaster is the application-specific library and is responsible for negotiating resources from the ResourceManager as per the client application's requirements and needs. The ApplicationMaster works with the NodeManager to execute and monitor the container and track the application's progress. The ApplicationMaster itself runs in one of the containers allocated by the ResourceManager, and the ResourceManager tracks the progress of the ApplicationMaster.

The ApplicationMaster provides scalability to the YARN framework, as the ApplicationMaster can provide a functionality that is much similar to that of the traditional ResourceManager, so the YARN cluster is able to scale with many hardware changes. Also, by moving all the application-specific code into the ApplicationMaster, YARN generalizes the system so that it can support multiple frameworks, just by writing the ApplicationMaster.

Summary

In this chapter, you learned how to use bundled applications that come with the YARN framework, how to develop the YARNClient and ApplicationMaster, the core parts of the YARN framework, how to submit an application to YARN, how to monitor an application, and the responsibilities of the ApplicationMaster.

In the next chapter, you will learn to write some real-time practical examples.

7
YARN Frameworks

It's the dawn of 2015, and big data is still in its booming stage. Many new start-ups and giants are investing a huge amount into developing POCs and new frameworks to cater to a new and emerging variety of problems. These frameworks are the new cutting-edge technologies or programming models that tend to solve the problems across industries in the world of big data. As the corporations are trying to use big data, they are facing a new and unique set of problems that they never faced before. Hence, to solve these new problems, many frameworks and programming models are coming onto the market.

YARN's support for multiple programming models and frameworks makes it ideal to be integrated with these new and emerging frameworks or programming models. With YARN taking responsibility for resource management and other necessary things (scheduling jobs, fault tolerance, and so on), it allows these new application frameworks to focus on solving the problems that they were specifically meant for.

At the time of writing this book, many new and emerging open source frameworks are already integrated with YARN.

In this chapter, we will cover the following frameworks that run on YARN:

- Apache Samza
- Storm on YARN
- Apache Spark
- Apache Tez
- Apache Giraph
- Hoya (HBase on YARN)
- KOYA (Kafka on YARN)

We will talk in detail about Apache Samza and Storm on YARN, where we will develop and run some sample applications. For other frameworks, we will have a brief discussion.

Apache Samza

Samza is an open source project from LinkedIn and is currently an incubation project at the Apache Software Foundation. Samza is a lightweight distributed stream-processing framework to do real-time processing of data. The version that is available for download from the Apache website is not the production version that LinkedIn uses.

Samza is made up of the following three layers:

- A streaming layer
- An execution layer
- A processing layer

Samza provides out-of-the-box support for all the preceding three layers:

- **Streaming**: This layer is supported by Kafka (another open source project from LinkedIn)
- **Execution**: supported by YARN
- **Processing**: supported by Samza API

The following three pieces fit together to form Samza:

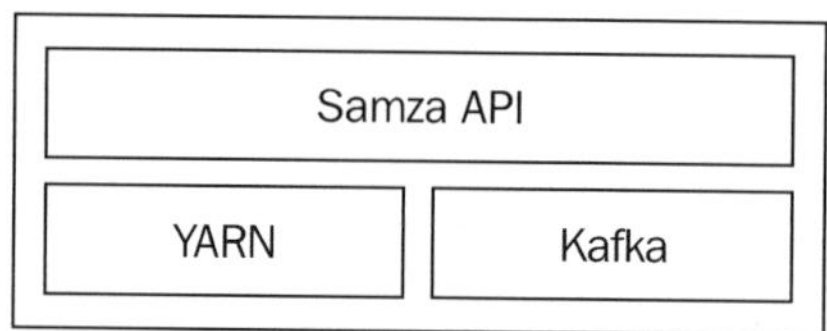

The following architecture should be familiar to anyone who has used Hadoop:

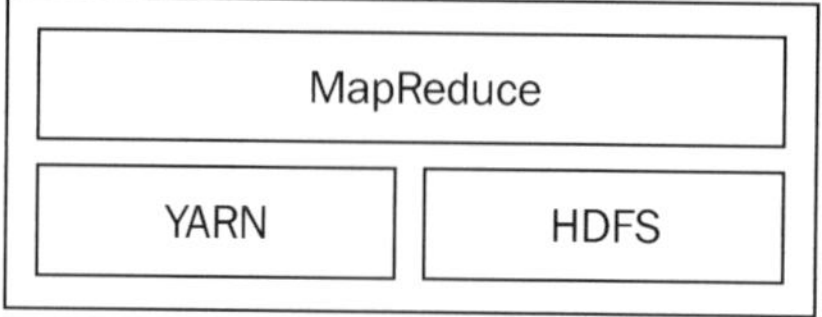

Before going into each of these three layers indepth, it should be noted that Samza's support is not limited to these systems. Both Samza's execution and streaming layers are pluggable and allow developers to implement alternatives as required.

Samza is a stream-processing system to run continuous computation on infinite streams of data.

Samza provides a system to process stream data from publish-subscribe systems such as Apache Kafka. The developer writes a stream-processing task and executes it as a Samza job. Samza then routes messages between the stream-processing tasks and the publish-subscribe systems that the messages are addressed to.

Samza works a lot like Storm, the Twitter-developed stream-processing technology, except that Samza runs on Kafka, LinkedIn's own messaging system. Samza was developed with a pluggable architecture, enabling developers to use the software with other messaging systems.

Apache Samza is basically a combination of the following technologies:

- **Kafka**: Samza uses Apache Kafka as its underlying message passing system
- **Apache YARN**: Samza also uses Apache YARN for task scheduling
- **ZooKeeper**: Both YARN and Kafka, in turn, rely on Apache ZooKeeper for coordination

More information is available on the official site at `http://samza.incubator.apache.org/`.

We will use the **hello-samza** project to develop a sample example to process some real-time stream processing.

We will write a Kafka producer using the Java Kafka APIs to publish a continuous stream of messages to a Kafka topic. Finally, we will write a Samza consumer using the Samza API to process these streams from the Kafka topic in real time. For simplicity, we will just print a message and record each time a message is received in the Kafka topic.

Writing a Kafka producer

Let's first write a Kafka producer to publish messages to a Kafka topic (named `storm-sentence`):

```
import java.io.BufferedReader;
import java.io.File;
import java.io.FileInputStream;
import java.io.FileNotFoundException;
import java.io.FileReader;
import java.io.IOException;
import java.io.PrintStream;
import java.util.Properties;
import kafka.javaapi.producer.Producer;
import kafka.producer.KeyedMessage;
import kafka.producer.ProducerConfig;

/**
 * A simple Java Class to publish messages into KAFKA.
 *
 *
 * @author nirmal.kumar
 *
 */
public class KafkaStringProducerService {
  public Producer<String, String> producer;

  public Producer<String, String> getProducer() {
    return this.producer;
  }

  public void setProducer(Producer<String, String> producer) {
    this.producer = producer;
  }

  public KafkaStringProducerService(Properties prop) {
    setProducer(new Producer(new ProducerConfig(prop)));
```

```
}

/**
 * Change the location of producer.properties accordingly in
   Line No. 123
 *
 * Load the producer.properties having following properties:
 * kafka.zk.connect=192.xxx.xxx.xxx
 * serializer.class=kafka.serializer.StringEncoder
 * producer.type=async
 * queue.buffering.max.ms=5000000
 * queue.buffering.max.messages=1000000
 * metadata.broker.list=192.xxx.xxx.xxx:9092
 *
 * @param filepath
 * @return
 */
private static Properties getConfiguartionProperties(String
  filepath) {
  File path = new File(filepath);
  Properties properties = new Properties();
  try {
    properties.load(new FileInputStream(path));
  } catch (FileNotFoundException e) {
    e.printStackTrace();
  } catch (IOException e) {
    e.printStackTrace();
  }
  return properties;
}

/**
 * Publishes each message to KAFKA
 *
 * @param input
 * @param ii
 */
public void execute(String input, int ii) {
```

```
      KeyedMessage data = new KeyedMessage("storm-sentence", input);

      this.producer.send(data);

      //Logs to System Console the no. of messages published (each
100000)
      if ((ii != 0) && (ii % 100000 == 0))
        System.out.println("$$$$$$$ PUBLISHED " + ii +
          " messages @ "
            + System.currentTimeMillis());
    }

    /**
     * Reads each line from the input message file
     *
     * @param file
     * @return
     * @throws IOException
     */
    private static String readFile(String file) throws IOException {
      BufferedReader reader = new BufferedReader(new
        FileReader(file));
      String line = null;
      StringBuilder stringBuilder = new StringBuilder();
      String ls = System.getProperty("line.separator");

      while ((line = reader.readLine()) != null) {
        stringBuilder.append(line);
        stringBuilder.append(ls);
      }

      return stringBuilder.toString();
    }

    /**
     * main method for invoking the Java application
     * Need to pass command line argument: the absolute file path
       containing String messages.
     *
     * @param args
```

```
  */
  public static void main(String[] args) {
    int ii = 0;
    int noOfMessages = Integer.parseInt(args[1]);

    String s = null;
    try {
      s = readFile(args[2]);
    } catch (IOException e) {
      e.printStackTrace();
    }

    /**
     * instantiate the Main class.
     * Change the location of producer.properties accordingly
     */
    KafkaStringProducerService service = new
      KafkaStringProducerService(
        getConfiguartionProperties("/home/cloud/producer.
properties"));

    System.out.println("******** START: Publishing " +
      noOfMessages
        + " messages @" + System.currentTimeMillis());

    while (ii <= noOfMessages) {
      // invoke the execute method to publish messages into KAFKA
      service.execute(s, ii);
      ii++;
    }
    System.out.println("####### END: Published " + noOfMessages
        + " messages @" + System.currentTimeMillis());
    try {
      service.producer.close();
    } catch (Exception e) {
      e.printStackTrace();
    }
  }
}
```

Create the `Producer.properties` file somewhere in `/home/cloud/producer.properties` and specify the location in the previous Kafka producer Java class.

The `Producer.properties` file will have the following information:

```
kfka.zk.connect=
serializer.class=kafka.serializer.StringEncoder
producer.type=async
queue.buffering.max.ms=5000000
queue.buffering.max.messages=1000000
metadata.broker.list=:9092
```

Writing the hello-samza project

Let's now write a Samza consumer and package it with the hello-samza project:

1. Download and build the hello-samza project. Check out the hello-samza project:

   `git clone git://git.apache.org/incubator-samza-hello-samza.git hello-samza`

   `cd hello-samza`

   The output of the preceding code can be seen here:

```
nirmal:pwd
/home/cloud/nirmal/samza
nirmal:git clone git://git.apache.org/incubator-samza-hello-samza.git hello-samza
Initialized empty Git repository in /home/cloud/nirmal/samza/hello-samza/.git/
remote: Counting objects: 385, done.
remote: Compressing objects: 100% (202/202), done.
remote: Total 385 (delta 158), reused 264 (delta 99)
Receiving objects: 100% (385/385), 4.82 MiB | 223 KiB/s, done.
Resolving deltas: 100% (158/158), done.
nirmal:ls
hello-samza
nirmal:cd hello-samza
nirmal:ls
bin  conf  LICENSE  pom.xml  README.md  samza-job-package  samza-wikipedia  wikipedia-raw.json
```

2. Next, we will write a Samza consumer using the Samza API to process these N messages from a Kafka topic. Got to `hello-samza/samza-wikipedia/src/main/java/samza/examples/wikipedia/task` and write the `YarnEssentialsSamzaConsumer.java` file as follows:

```
package samza.examples.wikipedia.task;

import java.io.PrintStream;
import java.util.Map;
import org.apache.samza.system.IncomingMessageEnvelope;
import org.apache.samza.task.MessageCollector;
import org.apache.samza.task.StreamTask;
import org.apache.samza.task.TaskCoordinator;

public class YarnEssentialsSamzaConsumer
  implements StreamTask
{
  public void process(IncomingMessageEnvelope envelope, MessageCollector collector, TaskCoordinator coordinator)
  {
        Map jsonObject = (Map)envelope.getMessage();
        System.out.println("********************** IN YarnEssentialsSamzaConsumer " + System.currentTimeMillis());
  }
}
```

3. After writing the Samza consumer class in the `hello-samza` project, you will need to build the project:

   mvn clean package

4. Create a `samza` directory inside the `deploy` directory:

   mkdir -p deploy/samza

5. Finally, create the Samza job package:

   tar -xvf ./samza-job-package/target/samza-job-package-0.7.0-dist.tar.gz -C deploy/samza

6. For Samza consumer properties, go to `/home/cloud/hello-samza/deploy/samza/config`.
7. Write a `samza-test-consumer.properties` file as follows:

```
# Job
job.factory.class=org.apache.samza.job.yarn.YarnJobFactory
job.name=test-Consumer

# YARN
yarn.package.path=file:/home/cloud/hello-samza/samza-job-package/target/samza-job-package-0.7.0-dist.tar.gz

# Task
task.class=samza.examples.wikipedia.task.YarnEssentialsSamzaConsumer
task.inputs=kafka.storm-sentence
task.window.ms=10000

# Serializers
serializers.registry.json.class=org.apache.samza.serializers.JsonSerdeFactory

# Systems
systems.kafka.samza.partition.manager=samza.stream.kafka.KafkaPartitionManager
systems.kafka.samza.consumer.factory=samza.stream.kafka.KafkaConsumerFactory

systems.kafka.samza.factory=org.apache.samza.system.kafka.KafkaSystemFactory
systems.kafka.samza.msg.serde=json
systems.kafka.consumer.zookeeper.connect=localhost:2181/
systems.kafka.consumer.auto.offset.reset=largest
systems.kafka.producer.metadata.broker.list=localhost:9092
```

This properties file will mainly contain the following information:

- `job.name`: This is the name of the Samza job
- `yarn.package.path`: This is the path of the Samza job package
- `task.class`: This is the class of the actual Samza consumer
- `task.inputs`: This is the Kafka topic name where the published will be read from
- `systems.kafka.consumer.zookeeper.connect`: This is the ZooKeeper-related information

Starting a grid

A Samza grid usually comprises three different systems: YARN, Kafka, and ZooKeeper. The `hello-samza` project comes with a script called `grid` to help you set up these systems. Start by running the following command:

```
bin/grid bootstrap
```

This command will download, install, and start ZooKeeper, Kafka, and YARN. It will also check out the latest version of Samza and build it. All the package files will be put in a subdirectory called `deploy` inside the `hello-samza` project's root folder. The result of the preceding command is shown here:

```
nirmal:ls
bin  conf  LICENSE  pom.xml  README.md  samza-job-package  samza-wikipedia  wikipedia-raw.json
nirmal:bin/grid bootstrap
Bootstrapping the system...
EXECUTING: stop kafka
Kafka is not installed. Run: bin/grid install kafka
EXECUTING: stop yarn
YARN is not installed. Run: bin/grid install yarn
EXECUTING: stop zookeeper
Zookeeper is not installed. Run: bin/grid install zookeeper
EXECUTING: install zookeeper
Downloading zookeeper-3.4.3.tar.gz...
  % Total    % Received % Xferd  Average Speed   Time    Time     Time  Current
                                 Dload  Upload   Total   Spent    Left  Speed
100 15.4M  100 15.4M    0     0   173k      0  0:01:31  0:01:31 --:--:--  252k
EXECUTING: install yarn
Downloading hadoop-2.2.0.tar.gz...
  % Total    % Received % Xferd  Average Speed   Time    Time     Time  Current
                                 Dload  Upload   Total   Spent    Left  Speed
100  104M  100  104M    0     0   227k      0  0:07:49  0:07:49 --:--:--  235k
EXECUTING: install kafka
Downloading kafka_2.9.2-0.8.1.1.tgz...
  % Total    % Received % Xferd  Average Speed   Time    Time     Time  Current
                                 Dload  Upload   Total   Spent    Left  Speed
 18 14.3M   18 2772k    0     0  89536      0  0:02:48  0:00:31  0:02:17  232k
```

The following screenshot shows that Zookeeper, YARN, and Kafka are being started:

```
EXECUTING: start zookeeper
JMX enabled by default
Using config: /home/cloud/nirmal/samza/hello-samza/deploy/zookeeper/bin/../conf/zoo.cfg
Starting zookeeper ... STARTED
EXECUTING: start yarn
starting resourcemanager, logging to /home/cloud/nirmal/samza/hello-samza/deploy/yarn/logs/yarn-cloud-resourcemanager-Impetus-942.impetus.co.in.out
log4j:ERROR Could not find value for key log4j.appender.RFA
log4j:ERROR Could not instantiate appender named "RFA".
log4j:ERROR Could not find value for key log4j.appender.RFA
log4j:ERROR Could not instantiate appender named "RFA".
starting nodemanager, logging to /home/cloud/nirmal/samza/hello-samza/deploy/yarn/logs/yarn-cloud-nodemanager-Impetus-942.impetus.co.in.out
log4j:ERROR Could not find value for key log4j.appender.RFA
log4j:ERROR Could not instantiate appender named "RFA".
log4j:ERROR Could not find value for key log4j.appender.RFA
log4j:ERROR Could not instantiate appender named "RFA".
EXECUTING: start kafka
nirmal:jps
```

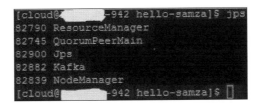

Once all the processes are up and running you can check the processes, as shown in this screenshot:

```
[cloud@        -942 hello-samza]$ jps
82790 ResourceManager
82745 QuorumPeerMain
82900 Jps
82882 Kafka
82839 NodeManager
[cloud@        -942 hello-samza]$
```

The YARN ResourceManager web UI will look like this:

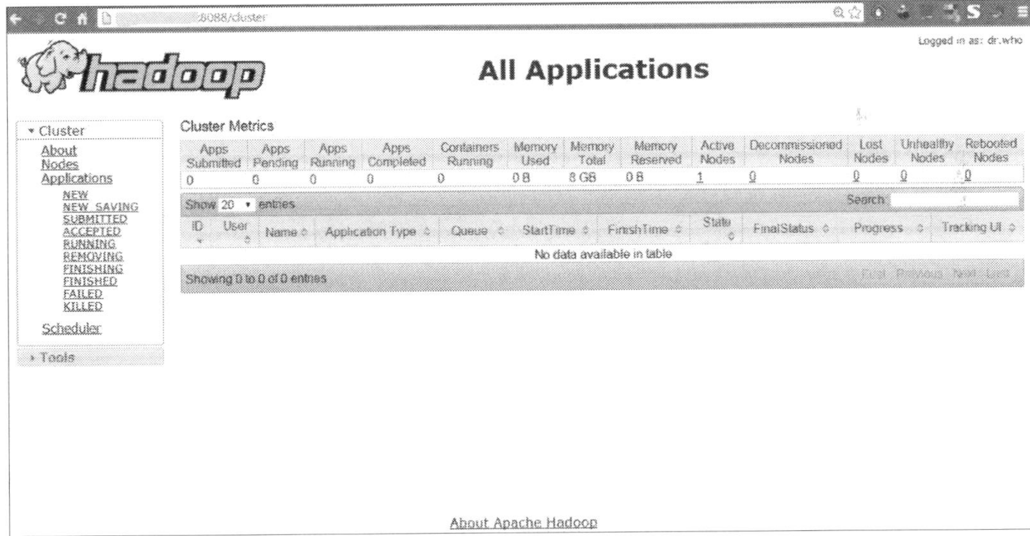

The YARN NodeManager web UI will look like this:

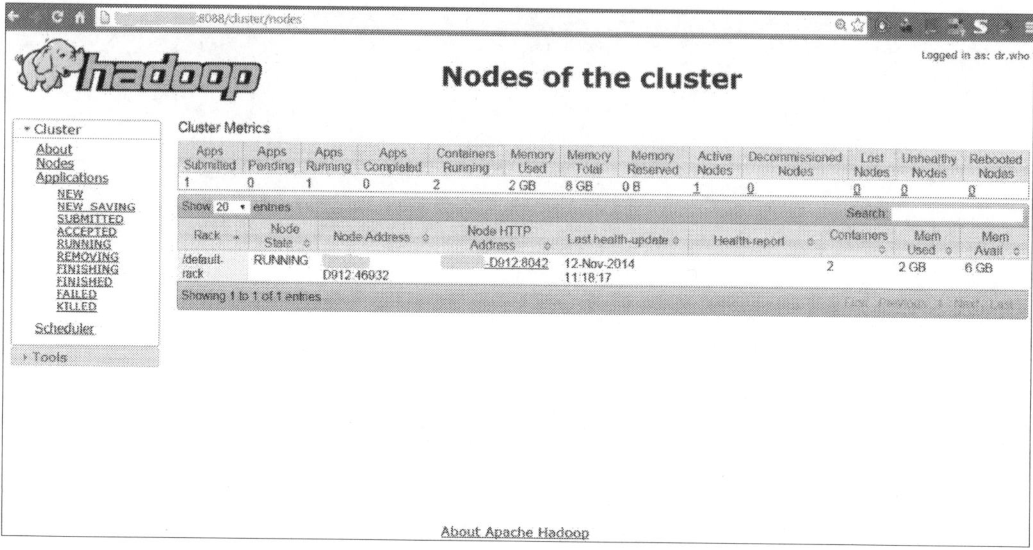

Since we started the grid, let's now deploy the Samza job to it:

```
deploy/samza/bin/run-job.sh --config-factory=org.apache.samza.config.
factories.PropertiesConfigFactory --config-path=file:/home/cloud/hello-
samza/deploy/samza/config/samza-test-consumer.properties
```

Check the application processes and RM UI. As you can see in the following screenshot, running the Samza job first creates a SamzaAppMaster and then a SamzaContainer to run the consumer that we wrote:

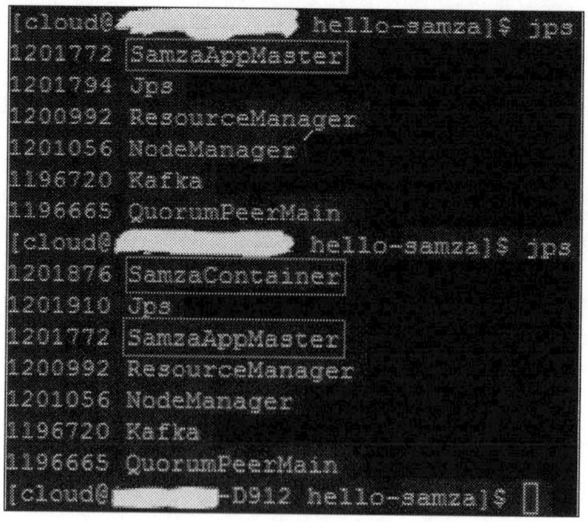

```
[cloud@ hello-samza]$ jps
1201772 SamzaAppMaster
1201794 Jps
1200992 ResourceManager
1201056 NodeManager
1196720 Kafka
1196665 QuorumPeerMain
[cloud@ hello-samza]$ jps
1201876 SamzaContainer
1201910 Jps
1201772 SamzaAppMaster
1200992 ResourceManager
1201056 NodeManager
1196720 Kafka
1196665 QuorumPeerMain
[cloud@ -D912 hello-samza]$
```

The ResourceManager web UI now shows the Samza application up and running:

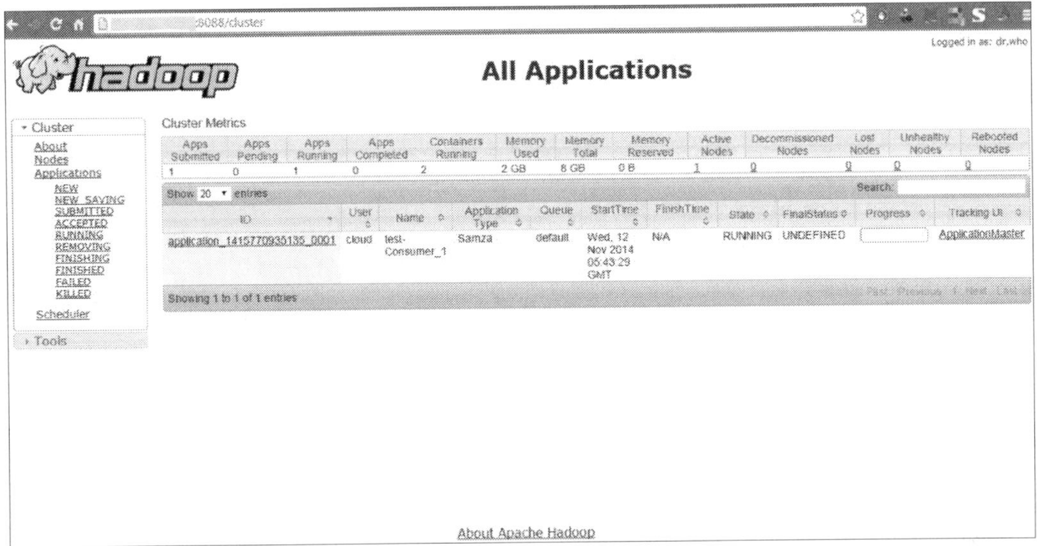

The ApplicationMaster UI looks as follows:

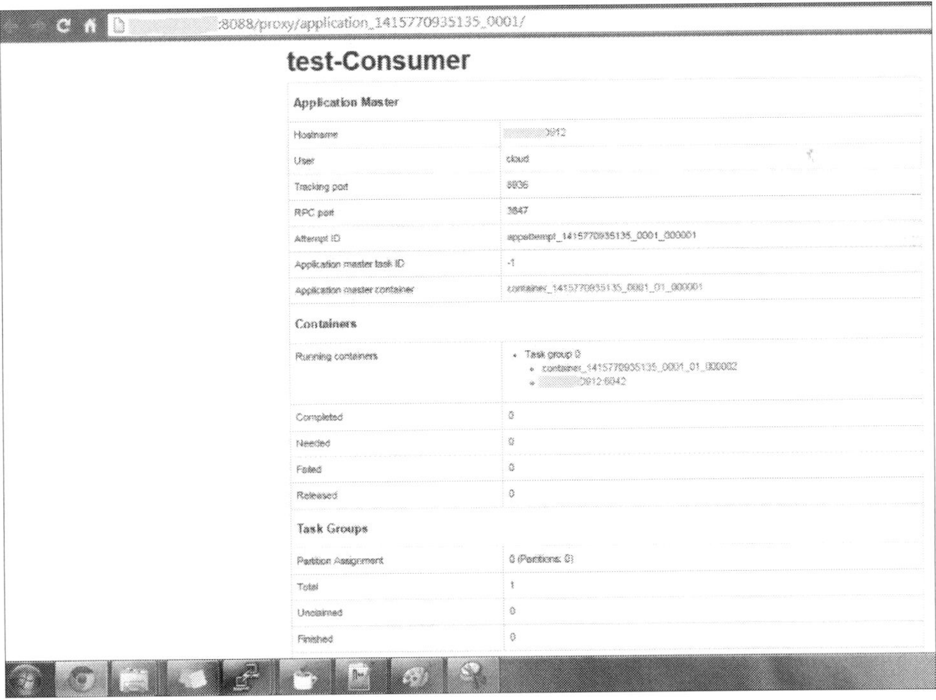

The following screenshot shows the ApplicationMaster UI interface:

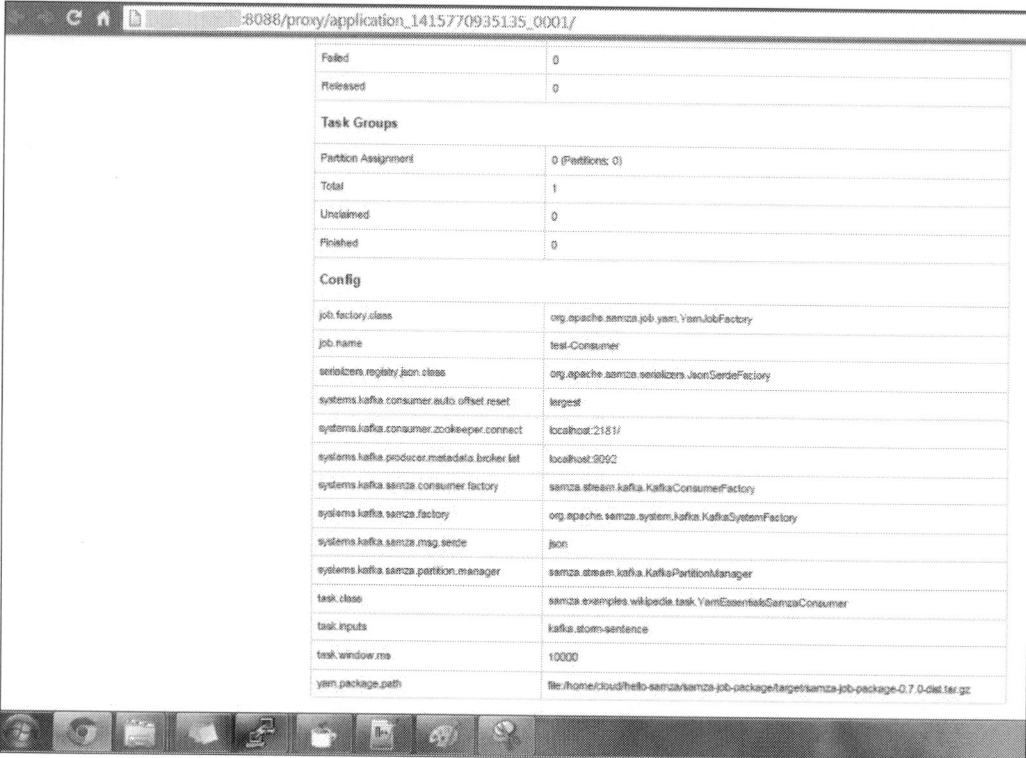

Since now our Samza consumer is up and running and listening for any messages in the Kafka topic (named `storm-sentence`), let's publish some messages to the Kafka topic using the Kafka producer we wrote initially. The following Java command is used to invoke the Kafka producer that has two command-line arguments:

- `N`: This is the number of times the message is published into Kafka
- `{pathOfFileNameHavingMessage}`: This is the actual string message

Create any file having a string message (`strmsg10K.txt`) and pass this file name and path as the second command-line argument to the Java command, as shown in the following screenshot:

```
[cloud@           ~]$ java -Xmx12g -jar Kafka0.8ProducerStorm0.8_10K_NO_Logs.jar com.      .kafka.producer.KafkaStringProducerService 200 strmsg10K.txt
log4j:WARN No appenders could be found for logger (kafka.utils.VerifiableProperties).
log4j:WARN Please initialize the log4j system properly.
SLF4J: Failed to load class "org.slf4j.impl.StaticLoggerBinder".
SLF4J: Defaulting to no-operation (NOP) logger implementation
SLF4J: See http://www.slf4j.org/codes.html#StaticLoggerBinder for further details.
******** START: Publishing 200 messages @1415771255735
######## END: Published 200 messages @1415771255742
```

As soon as these messages are published in the Kafka topic, the Samza consumer consumes it and prints the timestamp, as written in the Samza consumer code.

The result after checking the Samza consumer logs is as follows:

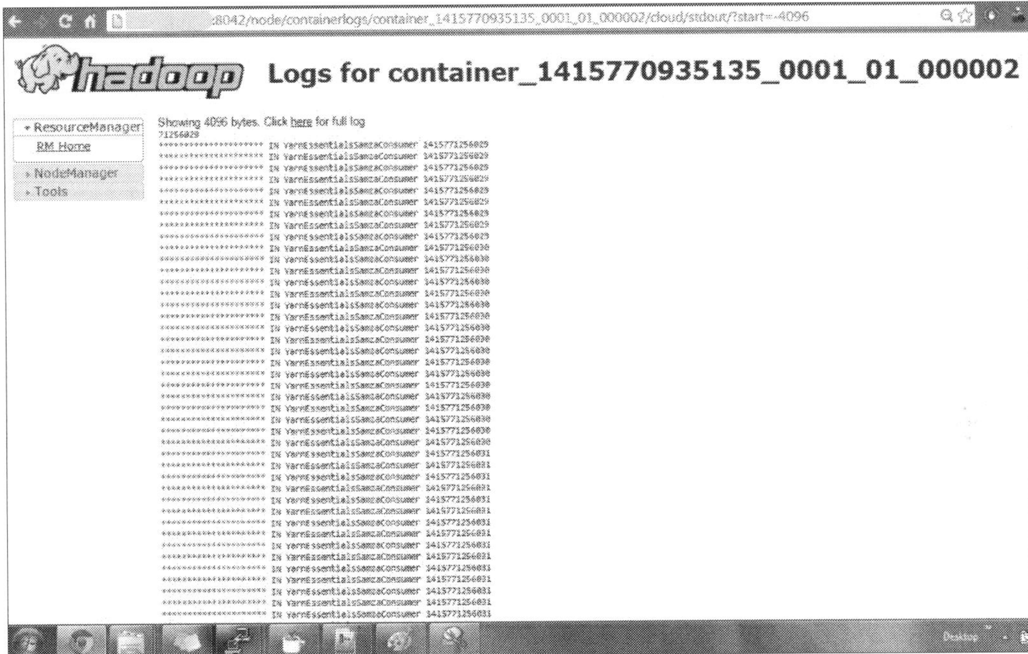

Storm-YARN

Apache Storm is an open source distributed real-time computation system from Twitter.

Storm helps in processing unbounded streams of data in a reliable manner. Storm can be used with any programming language. Some of the most common use cases of Storm are real-time analytics, real-time machine learning, continuous computation, ETL, and many more.

Storm-YARN is a project from Yahoo that enables the Storm cluster to be deployed and managed by YARN. Earlier, a separate cluster was needed for Hadoop and Storm.

One major benefit that comes with this integration is *elasticity*. Batch processing (Hadoop MapReduce) is usually done on the basis of need, and real-time processing (Storm) is an ongoing processing. When the Hadoop cluster is idle, you can leverage it for any real-time processing work.

In a typical real-time processing use case, constant and predictable loads are very rare. Storm, therefore, will need more resources during peak time when the load is greater. At peak time, Storm can steal resources from the batch jobs and give them back when the load is less.

This way, the overall resource utilization can scale up and down depending on the load and demand. This elasticity is, therefore, useful for utilizing the available resources on the basis of demand between real-time and batch processing.

Another benefit is that this integration reduces the physical distance of data transfers between Storm and Hadoop. Many applications use both Storm and Hadoop on separate clusters while sharing data between them (MapReduce). For such a scenario, Storm-YARN reduces network transfers, and in turn the total cost of acquiring the data, as they share the same cluster, as shown in the following image:

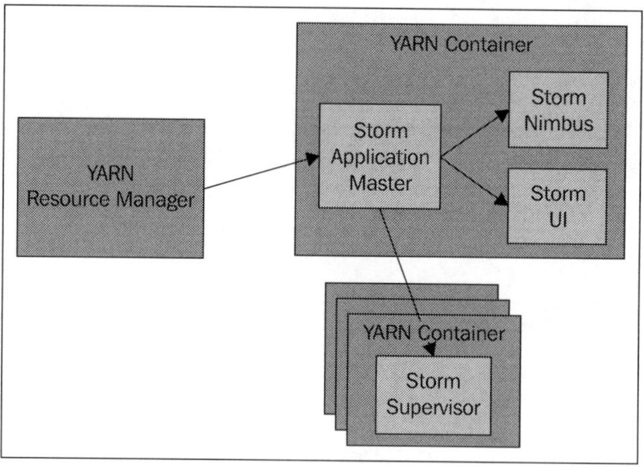

Referring to the preceding diagram, Storm-YARN asks YARN's ResourceManager to launch a Storm ApplicationMaster. The Storm ApplicationMaster then launches a Storm Nimbus server and a Storm UI server locally. It also uses YARN to allocate resources for the supervisors and finally launch them.

We will now install Storm-YARN on a Hadoop YARN cluster and deploy some Storm topologies to the cluster.

Prerequisites

The following are the prerequisites for Storm-YARN.

Hadoop YARN should be installed

Refer to the Hadoop YARN installation at http://hadoop.apache.org/docs/r2.4.1/hadoop-project-dist/hadoop-common/SingleCluster.html.

The Master Thrift service of Storm-on-YARN uses port 9000, and if Storm-YARN is launched from the NameNode, there will be a port crash.

In this case, you will need to change the port of the NameNode in your Hadoop installation. Typically, the following processes should be up and running in Hadoop:

```
nirmal@nirmal-Vostro-3560 ~/storm-on-yarn-poc/storm-yarn-master/lib $ jps
6008 QuorumPeerMain
6396 SecondaryNameNode
6136 NameNode
6233 DataNode
9405 NodeManager
10190 Jps
9296 ResourceManager
```

Apache ZooKeeper should be installed

At the time of writing this book, the Storm-on-YARN ApplicationMaster implementation does not include running Zookeeper on YARN. Therefore, it is presumed that there is a Zookeeper cluster already running to enable communication between Nimbus and workers.

There is an open issue that this thought at https://github.com/yahoo/storm-yarn/issues/22.

Installing Zookeeper is very straightforward and easy.

Refer to http://zookeeper.apache.org/doc/r3.3.3/zookeeperAdmin.html.

Setting up Storm-YARN

Storm-YARN is basically an implementation of the YARN client and ApplicationMaster for Storm.

The client gets a new application ID for Storm and submits the application, and the ApplicationMaster sets up the Storm components (Nimbus, Supervisor, and so on) on YARN using the containers that the ApplicationMaster requests from the ResourceManager.

Note that Storm-on-YARN is *not* a new implementation of Storm that works on YARN. Frameworks (that is Samza, Storm, Spark, Tez, and so on) themselves do not need to be modified to be able to run on YARN. Only the ApplicationMaster and the YARN client code need to be written for each of the frameworks so that they run on YARN as an application just like any other. Now, proceed with the following steps:

1. Clone the Storm-YARN repository from Git:

   ```
   cd storm-on-yarn-poc/
   git clone https://github.com/yahoo/storm-yarn.git
   cd storm-yarn
   ```

   The Storm client machine refers to the machine that will submit the YARN client and ApplicationMaster to the ResourceManager.

   As of now, there is single release of Storm-on-YARN from Yahoo that contains both Storm-YARN and Storm versions (0.9.0-wip21). The Storm release is present in the `lib` directory of the extracted Storm-on-YARN release.

2. Build Storm-YARN using Maven:

   ```
   mvn package or mvn package -DskipTests
   ```

3. We will get the following output:

   ```
   [INFO] Scanning for projects...
   [INFO]
   [INFO] Using the builder org.apache.maven.lifecycle.internal.
   builder.singlethreaded.SingleThreadedBuilder with a thread count
   of 1
   [INFO]
   [INFO] ------------------------------------------------------------
   -------------
   [INFO] Building storm-yarn 1.0-alpha
   ```

```
[INFO] ------------------------------------------------------------
-------------
[INFO]
[INFO] Compiling 5 source files to /home/nirmal/storm-on-yarn-poc/
storm-yarn-master/target/test-classes
[INFO]
[INFO] --- maven-jar-plugin:2.4:jar (default) @ storm-yarn ---
[INFO]
[INFO] --- maven-surefire-plugin:2.10:test (default-test) @ storm-
yarn ---
[INFO] Tests are skipped.
[INFO]
[INFO] --- maven-jar-plugin:2.4:jar (default-jar) @ storm-yarn ---
[INFO] ------------------------------------------------------------
-------------
[INFO] BUILD SUCCESS
[INFO] ------------------------------------------------------------
-------------
[INFO] Total time: 10.153 s
[INFO] Finished at: 2014-11-12T15:57:49+05:30
[INFO] Final Memory: 10M/118M
[INFO] ------------------------------------------------------------
-------------
 [INFO] Final Memory: 14M/152M
[INFO] -----------------------------------------------------
```

4. Next, you will need to copy the `storm.zip` file from `storm-yarn/lib` to HDFS. This is since Storm-on-YARN will deploy a copy of Storm code throughout all the nodes of the YARN cluster using HDFS. However, the location of where to fetch this copy of the Storm code is hardcoded into the Storm-on-YARN client. Copy the `storm.zip` file to HDFS using the following command:

```
hdfs dfs -mkdir -p /lib/storm/0.9.0-wip21
```

Alternatively, you can also use the following command:

```
hadoop fs - mkdir -p /lib/storm/0.9.0-wip21
hdfs dfs -put /home/nirmal/storm-on-yarn-poc/storm-yarn-master/
lib/storm.zip /lib/storm/0.9.0-wip21/storm.zip
```

You can also use the following command:

```
hadoop fs -put /home/nirmal/storm-on-yarn-poc/storm-yarn-master/
lib/storm.zip /lib/storm/0.9.0-wip21/storm.zip
```

The exact version of Storm might differ, in your case, from `0.9.0-wip21`.

5. Create a directory to hold our Storm configuration:

```
mkdir -p /home/nirmal/storm-on-yarn-poc/storm-data/

cp /home/nirmal/storm-on-yarn-poc/storm-yarn-master/lib/storm.zip
/home/nirmal/storm-on-yarn-poc/storm-data/

cd /home/nirmal/storm-on-yarn-poc/storm-data

unzip storm.zip
```

6. Add the following configuration in the `storm.yaml` file located at `/home/nirmal/storm-on-yarn-poc/storm-data/storm-0.9.0-wip21/conf`. You can change the following values as per your setup:
   - `storm.zookeeper.servers`: localhost
   - `nimbus.host`: localhost
   - `master.initial-num-supervisors`: 2
   - `master.container.size-mb`: 1024

7. Add the `storm-yarn/bin` folder to your path variable:

```
export PATH=$PATH:/home/nirmal/storm-on-yarn-poc/storm-data/storm-
0.9.0-wip21/bin:/home/nirmal/storm-on-yarn-poc/storm-yarn-master/
bin
```

8. Finally, launch Storm-YARN using the following command:

```
storm-yarn launch /home/nirmal/storm-on-yarn-poc/storm-data/storm-
0.9.0-wip21/conf/storm.yaml
```

Launching Storm-YARN executes the Storm-YARN client that gets an app ID from YARN's ResourceManager and starts running the Storm-YARN ApplicationMaster. The ApplicationMaster then starts the Nimbus, Workers, and Supervisor services. You will get an output similar to the one shown in the following screenshot:

```
nirmal@nirmal-Vostro-3560 ~/storm-on-yarn-poc/storm-yarn-master/lib $ storm-yarn launch /home/nirmal/storm-on-yarn-poc/storm-data/storm-0.9.0-wip21/conf/storm.yaml
SLF4J: Class path contains multiple SLF4J bindings.
SLF4J: Found binding in [jar:file:/home/nirmal/hadoop/HADOOP_versions/hadoop-2.3.0/share/hadoop/common/lib/slf4j-log4j12-1.7.5.jar!/org/slf4j/impl/StaticLoggerBinder.class]
SLF4J: Found binding in [jar:file:/home/nirmal/storm-on-yarn-poc/storm-data/storm-0.9.0-wip21/lib/logback-classic-1.0.6.jar!/org/slf4j/impl/StaticLoggerBinder.class]
SLF4J: See http://www.slf4j.org/codes.html#multiple_bindings for an explanation.
SLF4J: Actual binding is of type [org.slf4j.impl.Log4jLoggerFactory]
14/11/12 12:46:29 INFO client.RMProxy: Connecting to ResourceManager at /127.0.0.1:8032
14/11/12 12:46:29 WARN util.NativeCodeLoader: Unable to load native-hadoop library for your platform... using builtin-java classes where applicable
14/11/12 12:46:30 INFO yarn.StormOnYarn: Copy App Master jar from local filesystem and add to local environment
14/11/12 12:46:31 INFO yarn.StormOnYarn: Set the environment for the application master
14/11/12 12:46:31 INFO yarn.StormOnYarn: YARN CLASSPATH COMMAND = [[yarn, classpath]]
14/11/12 12:46:31 INFO yarn.StormOnYarn: YARN CLASSPATH = [/home/nirmal/hadoop/HADOOP_versions/hadoop-2.3.0/etc/hadoop:/home/nirmal/hadoop/HADOOP_versions/hadoop-2.3.0/etc/hadoop:/home/nirmal/hadoop/HADOOP_versions/hadoop-2.3.0/share/hadoop/common/lib/*:/home/nirmal/hadoop/HADOOP_versions/hadoop-2.3.0/share/hadoop/common/*:/home/nirmal/hadoop/HADOOP_versions/hadoop-2.3.0/share/hadoop/hdfs:/home/nirmal/hadoop/HADOOP_versions/hadoop-2.3.0/share/hadoop/hdfs/lib/*:/home/nirmal/hadoop/HADOOP_versions/hadoop-2.3.0/share/hadoop/hdfs/*:/home/nirmal/hadoop/HADOOP_versions/hadoop-2.3.0/share/hadoop/yarn/lib/*:/home/nirmal/hadoop/HADOOP_versions/hadoop-2.3.0/share/hadoop/yarn/*:/home/nirmal/hadoop/HADOOP_versions/hadoop-2.3.0/share/hadoop/mapreduce/lib/*:/home/nirmal/hadoop/HADOOP_versions/hadoop-2.3.0/share/hadoop/mapreduce/*:/home/nirmal/hadoop/HADOOP_versions/hadoop-2.3.0/contrib/capacity-scheduler/*.jar:/home/nirmal/hadoop/HADOOP_versions/hadoop-2.3.0/share/hadoop/yarn/*:/home/nirmal/hadoop/HADOOP_versions/hadoop-2.3.0/share/hadoop/yarn/lib/*]
14/11/12 12:46:31 INFO yarn.StormOnYarn: Using JAVA_HOME = [/opt/java/jdk1.7.0_51]
14/11/12 12:46:31 INFO yarn.StormOnYarn: Setting up app master command:[/opt/java/jdk1.7.0_51/bin/java, -Dstorm.home=./storm/storm-0.9.0-wip21/, -Dlogfile.name=<LOG_DIR>/master.log, com.yahoo.storm.yarn.MasterServer, 1><LOG_DIR>/stdout, 2><LOG_DIR>/stderr]
14/11/12 12:46:31 INFO impl.YarnClientImpl: Submitted application application_1415776508815_0001
application_1415776508815_0001
nirmal@nirmal-Vostro-3560 ~/storm-on-yarn-poc/storm-yarn-master/lib $ jps
```

9. We can retrieve the status of our application using the following YARN command:

   ```
   yarn application -list
   ```

   We will get the status of our application as follows:

```
nirmal@nirmal-Vostro-3560 ~/storm-on-yarn-poc/storm-yarn-master/lib $ yarn application -list
14/11/12 15:48:23 INFO client.RMProxy: Connecting to ResourceManager at /127.0.0.1:8032
14/11/12 15:48:24 WARN util.NativeCodeLoader: Unable to load native-hadoop library for your platform... using builtin-java classes where applicable
Total number of applications (application-types: [] and states: [SUBMITTED, ACCEPTED, RUNNING]):1
                Application-Id      Application-Name        Application-Type          User           Queue                   State             Final-State             Progress
        Tracking-URL
application_1415776508815_0001          Storm-on-Yarn                   YARN        nirmal         default                 RUNNING               UNDEFINED                  50%
                N/A
nirmal@nirmal-Vostro-3560 ~/storm-on-yarn-poc/storm-yarn-master/lib $
```

10. You can also see Storm-YARN running on the following ResourceManager web UI at `http://localhost:8088/cluster/`:

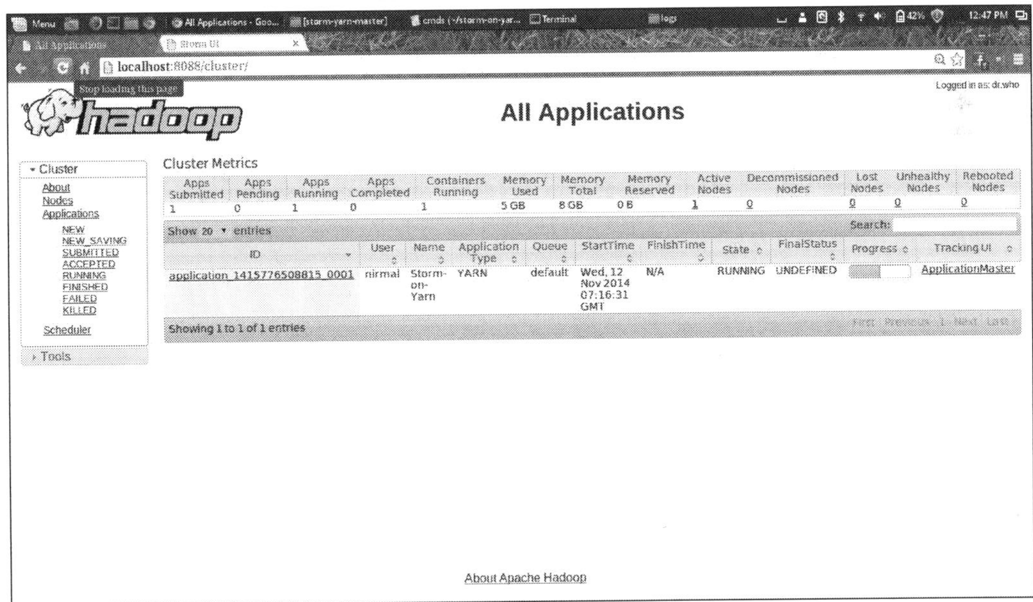

11. Nimbus should also be running now, and you should be able to see it through the Nimbus web UI at `http://localhost:7070/`. This looks as follows:

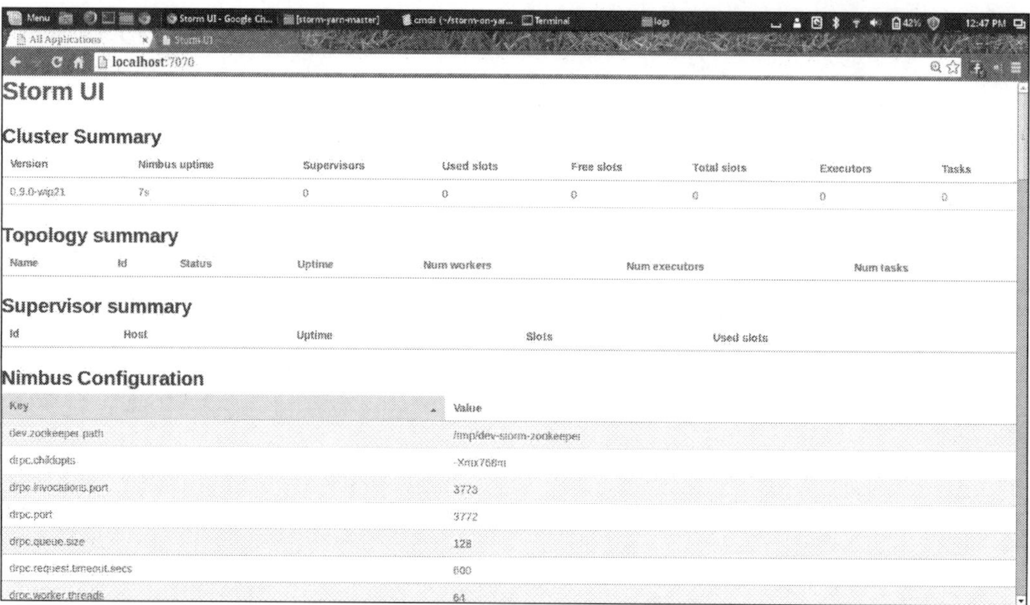

12. The following processes should be up and running:

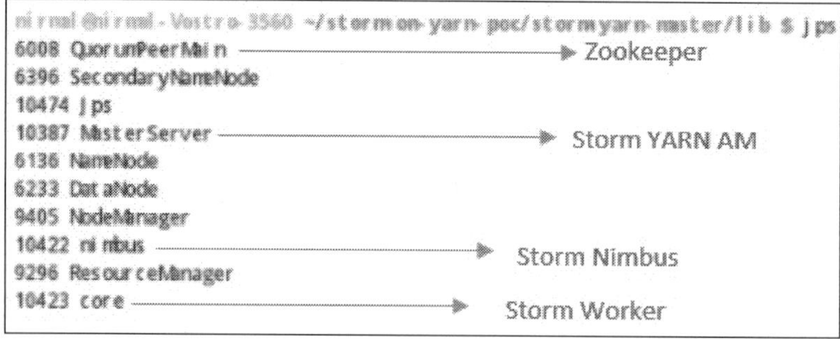

Getting the storm.yaml configuration of the launched Storm cluster

The machine that will use the Storm client command to submit a new topology to Storm needs the `storm.yaml` configuration file of the launched Storm cluster on YARN to be stored in `/home/nirmal/.storm/storm.yaml`.

Normally, when Storm is not run on YARN, this configuration file is manually edited, so you should know the IP addresses of the Storm components. However, since the location of where the Storm components will be run on YARN depends on the location of the allocated containers, Storm-on-YARN is responsible for setting `storm.yaml` for us. You can fetch this `storm.yaml` file from the running Storm-on-YARN:

```
$ cd
$ mkdir .storm/
$ storm-yarn getStormConfig -appId (check the appId on the YARN
application UI at port 8088) -output /home/nirmal/.storm/storm.yaml
```

Building and running Storm-Starter examples

In this section, we will see how to get the example code from GitHub, build it using Maven, and finally, run the examples. To perform these tasks, you'll have to execute the following steps:

1. Get the code from GitHub. We will use the `storm-starter` from GitHub:
   ```
   git clone https://github.com/nathanmarz/storm-starter
   Cloning into 'storm-starter'...
   remote: Counting objects: 756, done.
   remote: Total 756 (delta 0), reused 0 (delta 0)
   Receiving objects: 100% (756/756), 171.81 KiB | 56.00 KiB/s, done.
   Resolving deltas: 100% (274/274), done.
   Checking connectivity... done
   ```
2. Next, go to the downloaded `storm-starter` directory:
   ```
   cd storm-starter/
   ```

3. Check the content using the following commands:

```
ls -ltr
-rw-r--r-- 1 nirmal nirmal 171 Nov 12 12:58 README.markdown
-rw-r--r-- 1 nirmal nirmal 5047 Nov 12 12:58 m2-pom.xml
drwxr-xr-x 3 nirmal nirmal 4096 Nov 12 12:58 multilang
-rw-r--r-- 1 nirmal nirmal 580 Nov 12 12:58 LICENSE
drwxr-xr-x 4 nirmal nirmal 4096 Nov 12 12:58 src
-rw-r--r-- 1 nirmal nirmal 929 Nov 12 12:58 project.clj
drwxr-xr-x 3 nirmal nirmal 4096 Nov 12 12:58 test
-rw-r--r-- 1 nirmal nirmal 8042 Nov 12 12:58 storm-starter.iml
```

4. Build the `storm-starter` project using Maven:

```
mvn -f m2-pom.xml package or mvn -f m2-pom.xml package -DskipTests
```

5. You will see an output similar to the following commands:

```
[INFO] Scanning for projects...
[INFO] Using the builder org.apache.maven.lifecycle.internal.
builder.singlethreaded.SingleThreadedBuilder with a thread count
of 1
[INFO]
[INFO] -------------------------------------------------------------
------------
[INFO] Building storm-starter 0.0.1-SNAPSHOT
[INFO] -------------------------------------------------------------
------------
[INFO] META-INF/MANIFEST.MF already added, skipping
[INFO] META-INF/ already added, skipping
[INFO] META-INF/maven/ already added, skipping
[INFO] Building jar: /home/nirmal/storm-on-yarn-poc/storm-starter/
target/storm-starter-0.0.1-SNAPSHOT-jar-with-dependencies.jar
[INFO] META-INF/MANIFEST.MF already added, skipping
[INFO] META-INF/ already added, skipping
[INFO] META-INF/maven/ already added, skipping
[INFO] -------------------------------------------------------------
------------
[INFO] BUILD SUCCESS
```

```
[INFO] ------------------------------------------------------------
-------------
[INFO] Total time: 05:21 min
[INFO] Finished at: 2014-11-12T13:05:40+05:30
[INFO] Final Memory: 30M/191M
[INFO] ------------------------------------------------------------
-------------
```

6. After the build is successful, you will see the following JAR file being created under the target directory:

   `storm-starter-0.0.1-SNAPSHOT-jar-with-dependencies.jar`

7. Run the Storm topology example on the Storm-YARN cluster:

   ```
   storm jar storm-starter-0.0.1-SNAPSHOT-jar-with-dependencies.jar
   storm.starter.WordCountTopology word-count-topology
   ```

   The output can be seen in the following screenshot:

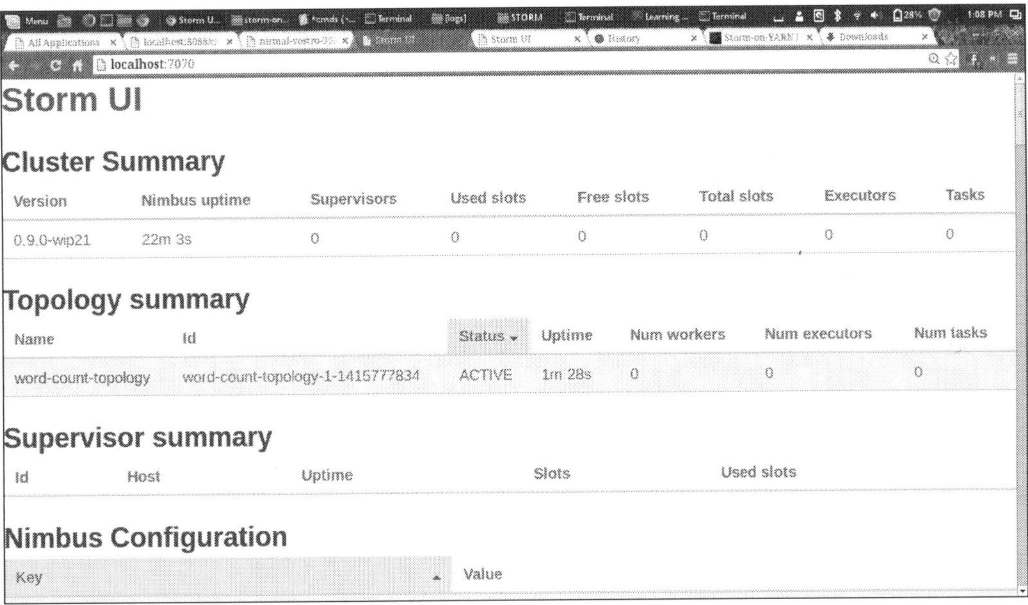

8. Click on the topology, as shown in the following screenshot:

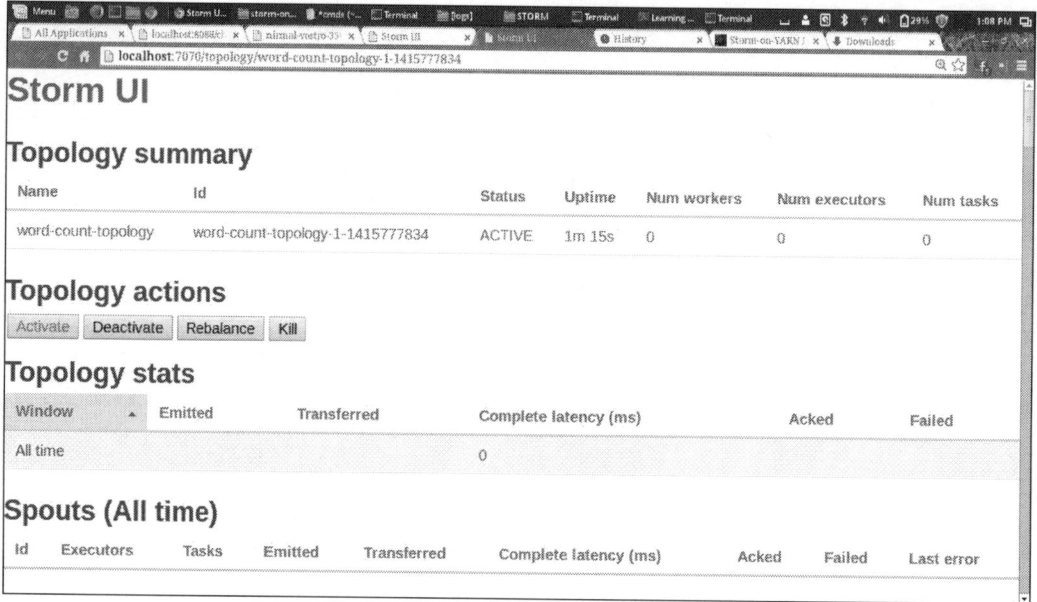

Apache Spark

Apache Spark is a fast and general engine for large-scale data processing. It was originally developed in 2009 in UC Berkeley's AMPLab and open sourced in 2010.

The main features of Spark are as follows:

- **Speed**: Spark enables applications in Hadoop clusters to run up to 100x faster in memory and 10x faster even when running on disk.
- **Ease of use**: Spark lets you quickly write applications in Java, Scala, or Python. You can use it interactively to query big datasets from the Scala and Python shells.
- **Runs everywhere**: Spark runs on Hadoop, Mesos, in standalone mode, or in the cloud. It can access diverse data sources, including HDFS, Cassandra, HBase, and S3. You can run Spark readily using its standalone cluster mode, on EC2, or run it on Hadoop YARN or Apache Mesos. It can read from HDFS, HBase, Cassandra, and any Hadoop data source.
- **Generality**: Spark powers a stack of high-level tools, including Spark SQL, MLlib for machine learning, GraphX, and Spark Streaming. You can combine these frameworks seamlessly in the same application.

Why run on YARN?

YARN enables Spark to run in a single cluster alongside other frameworks, such as Tez, Storm, HBase, and others. This avoids the need to create and manage separate and dedicated Spark clusters.

Typically, customers want to run multiple workloads on a single dataset in a single cluster. YARN, as a generic resource management and single data platform for all different frameworks/engines, makes it happen.

YARN's built-in multitenancy support allows dynamic and optimal sharing of the same shared cluster resources between different frameworks that run on YARN.

YARN has pluggable schedulers to categorize, isolate, and prioritize workloads.

Apache Tez

Apache Tez is part of the Stinger initiative led by Hortonworks to make the Hive enterprise ready and suitable for interactive SQL queries. The Tez design is based on research done by Microsoft on parallel and distributed computing.

Tez entered the Apache Incubator in February 2013 and graduated to a top-level project in July 2014.

Tez is basically an embeddable and extensible framework to build high-performance batch and interactive data-processing applications that need to integrate easily with YARN.

Confusion often arises when Tez is thought of as an engine. Tez is *not* a general-purpose engine, but more of a framework for tools to express their purpose-built needs. Tez, for example, enables Hive, Pig, and others to build their own purpose-built engines and embed them in those technologies to express their purpose-built needs. Projects such as Hive, Pig, and Cascading now have significant improvements in response times when they use Tez instead of MapReduce.

Tez generalizes the MapReduce paradigm to a more powerful framework based on expressing computations as a dataflow graph. Tez exists to address some of the limitations of MapReduce. For example, in a typical MapReduce, a lot of temporary data is stored (such as each mapper's output, which is a disk I/O), which is an overhead. In the case of Tez, this disk I/O of temporary data is saved, thereby resulting in higher performance compared to the MapReduce model.

Also, Tez can adjust the parallelism of reduce tasks at runtime, depending on the actual data size coming out of the previous task. On the other hand, in MapReduce the number of reducers is static and has to be decided by the user before the job is submitted to the cluster.

The processing done by multiple MapReduce jobs can now be done by a single Tez job, as follows:

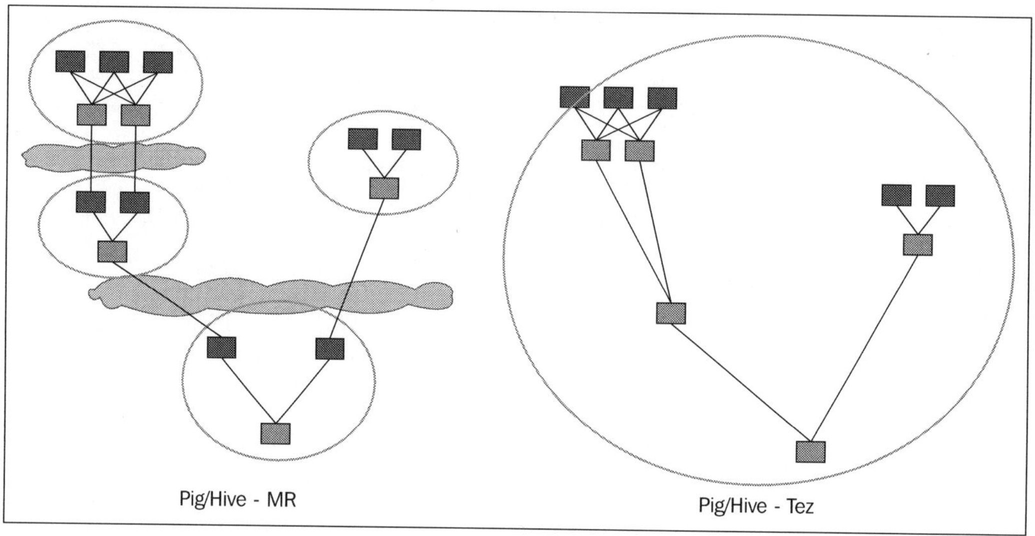

Referring to the preceding diagram, earlier (with PIG/HIVE), we used to need multiple M/R jobs to do some processing. However, now, in Tez, a single M/R job does the same, that is, the reducers (the green boxes) of the previous step feed the mappers (the blue boxes) of the next step.

The preceding image is taken from `http://www.infoq.com/articles/apache-tez-saha-murthy`.

Tez is not meant directly for end users; in fact, it enables developers to build end-user applications with much better performance and flexibility. Traditionally, Hadoop has been a batch-processing platform to process large amounts of data. However, there are a lot of use cases for near-real-time performance of query processing. There are also several workloads, such as machine learning, that do not fit into the MapReduce paradigm. Tez helps Hadoop address these use cases.

Tez provides an expressive dataflow-definition API that lets developers create their own unique **data-processing graphs** (**DAGs**) to represent their applications' data-processing flows. Once the developer defines a flow, Tez then provides additional APIs to inject custom business logic that will run in that flow. These APIs then combine inputs (that read data), outputs (that write data), and processors (that process data) to process the flow.

Tez can also run any existing MR job without any modification. For more information on Tez, refer to `http://tez.apache.org/`.

Apache Giraph

Apache Giraph is a graph-processing system that uses the MapReduce model to process graphs. Currently, it is in incubation at the Apache Software Foundation.

It is based on Google's Pregel, which is used to calculate page rank.

Currently, Giraph is being used by Facebook, Twitter, and LinkedIn to create social graphs of their users. Both Giraph and Pregel are based on the **Bulk Synchronous Parallel** (**BSP**) model of distributed computation, which was introduced by Leslie Valiant.

Support for YARN is from release 1.1.0. For more information, refer to the official site at `http://giraph.apache.org/`.

HOYA (HBase on YARN)

Hoya is basically running HBase on YARN. It is currently hosted on Github, but there are plans to move it to the Apache Foundation.

Hoya creates HBase clusters on top of YARN. It does this with a client application called Hoya client; this application creates the persistent configuration files, sets up the HBase cluster XML files, and then asks YARN to create an ApplicationMaster, which is the Hoya AM here.

For more information, refer to `https://github.com/hortonworks/hoya`, `http://hortonworks.com/blog/introducing-hoya-hbase-on-yarn/` and `http://hortonworks.com/blog/hoya-hbase-on-yarn-application-architecture/`.

KOYA (Kafka on YARN)

On November 5, 2014, DataTorrent, a company founded by ex-Yahoo!, announced a new project to bring the fault-tolerant, high-performance, scalable Apache Kafka messaging system to YARN.

The so-called **Kafka on YARN (KOYA)** project plans to leverage YARN for Kafka broker management, automatic broker recovery, and more. Planned features include a fully-HA ApplicationMaster, sticky allocation of containers (so that a restart can access local data), a web interface for Kafka, and more.

The expected release to the open source community is somewhere in Q2 2015.

More information is available at `https://www.datatorrent.com/introducing-koya-apache-kafka-on-apache-hadoop-2-0-yarn/`.

Summary

This chapter talked about the different frameworks and programming models that can be run on YARN. We discussed Apache Samza and Storm on YARN in detail.

With the wide acceptance of YARN in the industry, more and more frameworks will support YARN, taking complete advantage of YARN's generic features.

We looked at the existing frameworks that are integrated with YARN at the moment.

There is a lot more work going on in the industry to make existing and new applications run on YARN.

In *Chapter 8, Failures in YARN*, we will discuss how faults, failures at various levels, are handled in YARN.

8
Failures in YARN

Dealing with failures in distributed systems is comparatively more challenging and time consuming. Also, the Hadoop and YARN frameworks run on commodity hardware and cluster size nowadays; this size can vary from several nodes to several thousand nodes. So handling failure scenarios and dealing with ever-growing scaling issues is very important. In this section, we will focus on failures in the YARN framework: the causes of failures and how to overcome them.

In this chapter, we will cover the following topics:

- ResourceManager failures
- ApplicationMaster failures
- NodeManager failures
- Container failures
- Hardware failures

We will be dealing with the root causes of these failures and the solutions to them.

ResourceManager failures

In the initial versions of the YARN framework, ResourceManager failures meant a total cluster failure, as it was a single point of failure. The ResourceManager stores the state of the cluster, such as the metadata of the submitted application, information on cluster resource containers, information on the cluster's general configurations, and so on. Therefore, if the ResourceManager goes down because of some hardware failure, then there is no way to avoid manually debugging the cluster and restarting the ResourceManager. During the time the ResourceManager is down, the cluster is unavailable, and once it gets restarted, all jobs would need a restart, so the half-completed jobs lose any data and need to be restarted again. In short, a restart of the ResourceManager used to restart all the running ApplicationMasters.

The latest versions of YARN address this problem in two ways. One way is by creating an active-passive ResourceManager architecture, so that when one goes down, another becomes active and takes responsibility for the cluster. The ResourceManager RM state can be seen in the following image:

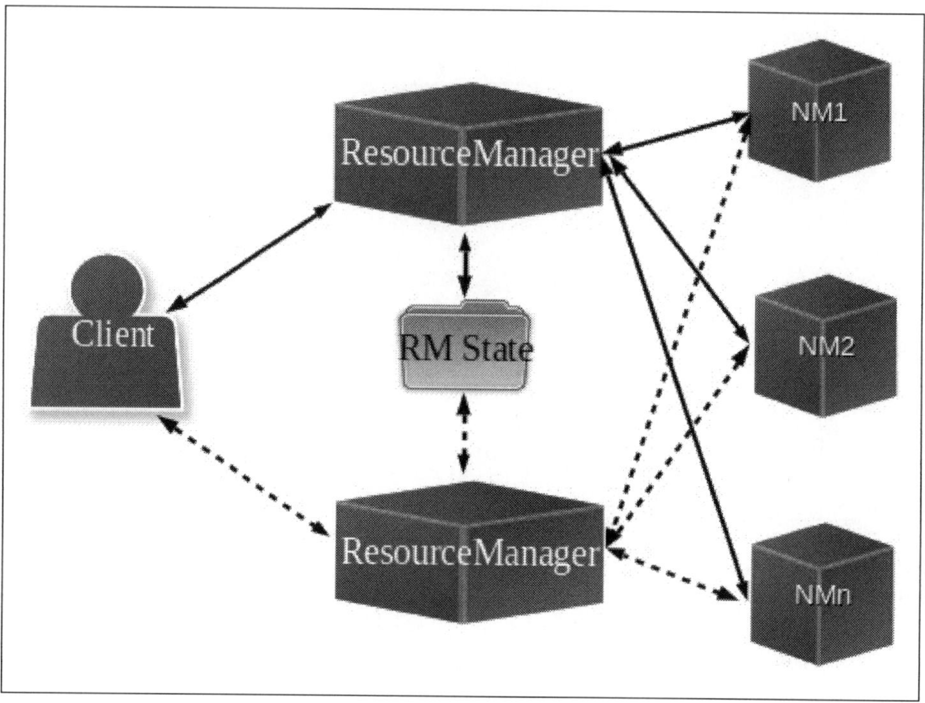

Another way is by using the Zookeeper ResourceManager quorum, so that the ResourceManager state is stored externally over the Zookeeper, and one ResourceManager is in an active state and one or more ResourceManagers are in passive mode, waiting for something to happen that brings them to an active state. The ResourceManager's state can be seen in the following image:

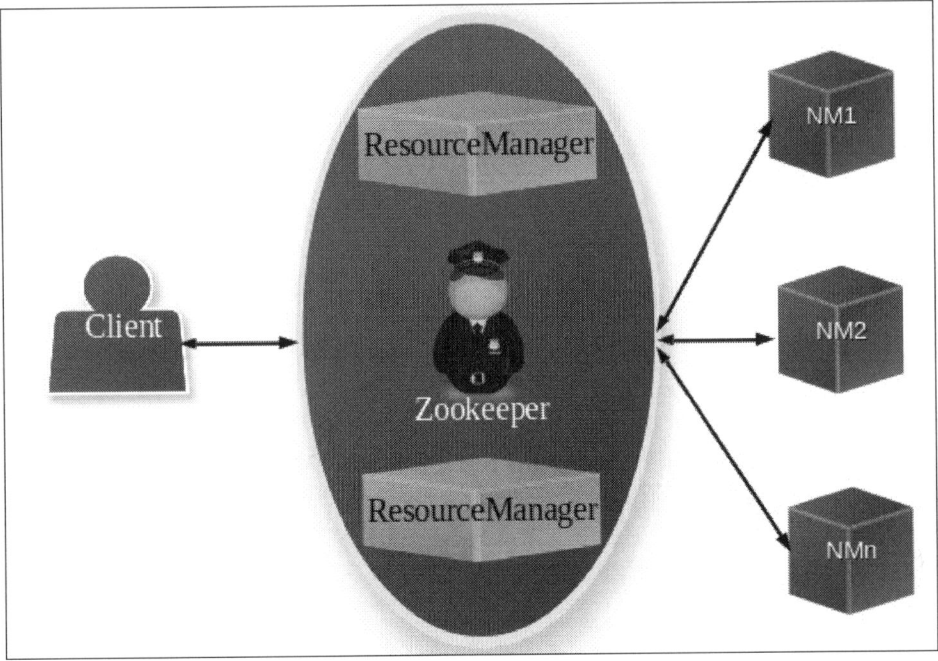

In the preceding diagram, you can see that the ResourceManager's state is managed by the Zookeeper. Whenever there is a failure condition, the ResourceManager's state is shared with the passive ResourceManager(s) to change to an active state and take over responsibility for the cluster, without any downtime.

ApplicationMaster failures

To recover the application's state after its restart because of an ApplicationMaster failure is the responsibility of the ApplicationMaster itself. When the ApplicationMaster fails, the ResourceManager simply starts another container with a new ApplicationMaster running in it for another application attempt. It is the responsibility of the new ApplicationMaster to recover the state of the older ApplicationMaster, and this is possible only when ApplicationMasters persist their states in the external location so that it can be used for future reference. Any ApplicationMaster can run any application from scratch instead of recovering its state and rerunning again.

For example, an ApplicationMaster can recover its completed jobs. However, if the jobs that are running and completed during the ApplicationMaster's recovery time frame get halted for some reason, their state will be discarded and the ApplicationMaster will simply rerun them from scratch.

The YARN framework is capable of rerunning the ApplicationMaster a specified number of times and recovering the completed tasks.

NodeManager failures

Almost all nodes in the cluster runs a NodeManager service daemon. The NodeManager takes care of executing a certain part of a YARN job on every individual machine, while other parts are executed on other nodes. For a 1000 node YARN cluster, there are probably around 999 node managers running. So node managers are indeed a per-node agent and takes care of the individual nodes distributed in the cluster.

If a Node Manager fails, the ResourceManager detects this failure using a time-out (that is, stops receiving the heartbeats from the NodeManager). The ResourceManager then removes the NodeManager from its pool of available NodeManagers. It also kills all the containers running on that node & reports the failure to all running AMs. AMs are then responsible for reacting to node failures, by redoing the work done by any containers running on that node during the fault.

If the fault causing the time-out is transient then the Node Manager will resynchronizes with the ResourceManager. On the similar lines if a new Node Manager joins the cluster, the ResourceManager notifies all ApplicationMasters about the availability of new resources.

Container failures

Whenever a container finishes, the ApplicationMaster is informed of this event by the ResourceManager. So the ApplicationMaster interprets that the container status received through the ResourceManager is the success or failure from container exit status. The ApplicationMaster handles the failures of the job containers.

It is the responsibility of the application frameworks to manage the container's failures, and the responsibility of the YARN framework is to provide information to the application framework. As a part of allocating the API's response, the ResourceManager collects information on the finished containers from the ApplicationMaster, as the containers return all this information to the corresponding ApplicationMaster. It is the responsibility of the ApplicationMaster to validate the container's status, exit code, and diagnostic information and appropriate action on it, for example when the MapReduce ApplicationMaster retries the map and reduce tasks by requesting new containers, until the configured number of tasks fail for a single job.

To address container allocation failure scenarios, the ResourceManager collects container information by executing the Allocate call, and the AllocateResponse usually does not return any containers. However, the Allocate call should be made periodically to ensure that all containers are assigned. When the container arrives, it is for sure that the framework will have sufficient resources, and the ApplicationMaster will not receive more containers than it asked for. Also, the ApplicationMaster can make separate container requests, ResourceRequests, typically one per second.

Hardware Failures

As the Hadoop and YARN frameworks use commodity hardware for the cluster setup and scaling from several nodes to several thousand nodes, all the components of Hadoop or YARN are designed on the assumption that hardware failures are very common. Therefore, these failures would be automatically handled by the framework so that important data is not lost because of them. For this, Hadoop provides data replication across the nodes/racks so that even if the whole rack fails, data would be recovered from another node on another rack, and jobs would be restarted over another replica dataset to compute the results.

Summary

In this chapter, we discussed YARN failure scenarios and how these are addressed in the YARN framework. In the next chapter, we will be focusing on alternative solutions for the YARN framework. We will also see a brief overview of the most common frameworks that are closely related to YARN.

9

YARN – Alternative Solutions

During the development of YARN, many other organizations simultaneously identified the limitations of Hadoop 1.x and were actively involved in developing alternative solutions.

This chapter will briefly talk about such alternate solutions and compare them to YARN. Among the most common frameworks that are closely related to YARN are:

- Mesos
- Omega
- Corona

Mesos

Mesos was originally developed at the University of California at Berkeley and later became open source under the **Apache Software Foundation**.

Mesos can be thought of as a highly-available and fault-tolerant operating system kernel for your clusters. It's a cluster resource manager that provides efficient resource isolation and sharing across multiple diverse cluster-computing or frameworks.

Mesos can be compared to YARN in some aspects but a complete quantitative comparison is literally not possible.

We will talk about the architecture of Mesos and compare some of the architectural differences with respect to YARN. This way we will have a high level understanding of the main difference between the two frameworks.

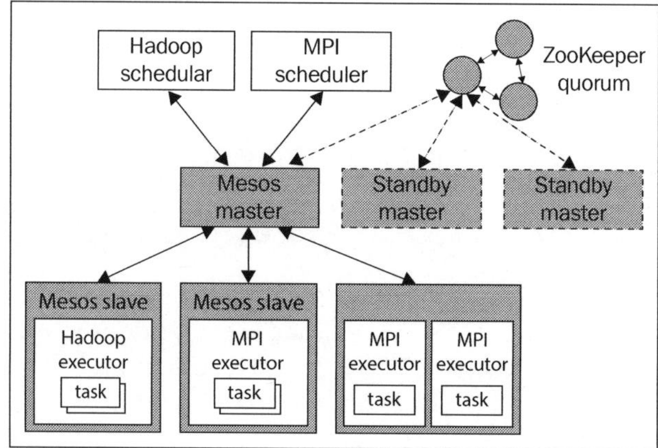

The preceding figure shows the main components of Mesos. It basically consists of a master process that manages slave processes running on each cluster node and mesos applications (also called frameworks) that run tasks on these slaves.

For more information please refer to the official site at `http://mesos.apache.org/`.

Here are the high-level differences between Mesos and YARN:

Mesos	**YARN**
Mesos uses Linux container groups (`http://lxc.sourceforge.net`). Linux container groups are a stronger isolation but may have some additional overhead.	YARN uses simple Unix processes.
Mesos is primarily written in C++.	YARN is primarily written in Java with bits of native code.
Mesos supports both memory and CPU scheduling.	Currently, YARN only supports memory scheduling (for example, you request x containers of y MB each), but there are plans to extend it to other resources such as network and disk I/O resources.

Mesos	YARN
Mesos introduces a distributed two-level scheduling mechanism called resource offers. Mesos decides how many resources to offer each framework, while frameworks decide which resources to accept and which computations to run on them.	YARN has a request-based approach. It allows the ApplicationMaster to ask for resources based on various criteria, including locations, and also allows the requester to modify future requests based on what was given and on the current usage.
Mesos leverages a pool of central schedulers (for example, classic Hadoop or MPI).	YARN on the other hand has a per job scheduler. Although YARN enables late binding of containers to tasks, where each individual job can perform local optimizations, the per-job ApplicationMaster might result in greater overhead than the Mesos approach.

Omega

Omega is Google's next generation cluster management system.

Omega is specifically focused on a **cluster scheduling architecture** that uses parallelism, shared state, and optimistic concurrency control.

From the past experience, Google noticed that as the clusters and their workloads increase, the scheduler is at risk of becoming a scalability bottleneck.

Google's production job scheduler has experienced all of this. Over the years, it has evolved into a complicated, sophisticated system that is hard to change.

A schematic overview of the scheduling architectures can be seen in the following figure:

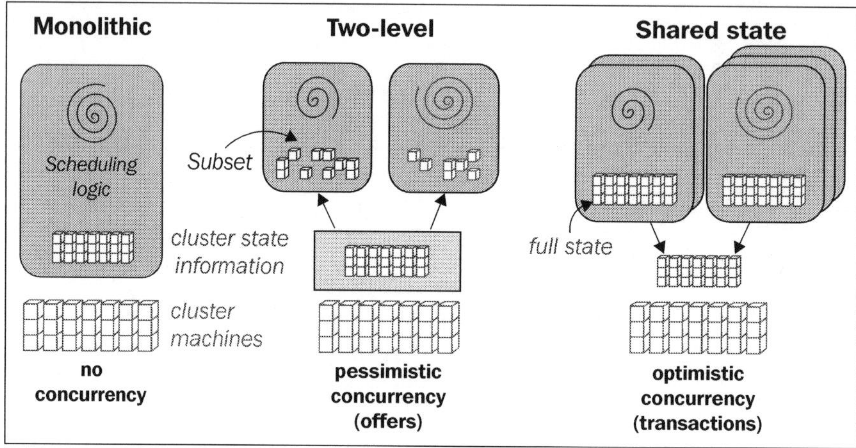

- contrib project to Hadoop 0.20 branch and is not a very large code base.
- Corona is integrated with the fair-scheduler.
- YARN is more interested in the capacity scheduler.

Google identified the following two prevalent scheduler architectures shown in the preceding figure:

- **Monolithic schedulers**: This uses a single, centralized scheduling algorithm for all jobs (our existing scheduler is one of these). They do not make it easy to add new policies and specialized implementations, and may not scale up to the cluster sizes one is planning for in the future.
- **Two-level schedulers**: This will have a single active resource manager that offers compute resources to multiple parallel, independent *scheduler frameworks*, as in Mesos and **Hadoop On Demand** (**HOD**). Their architectures do appear to provide flexibility and parallelism, but in practice their conservative resource visibility and locking algorithms limit both, and make it hard to place difficult to-schedule "picky" jobs or to make decisions that require access to the state of the entire cluster.

The solution is **Omega**—a new parallel scheduler architecture built around the shared state, using lock-free optimistic concurrency control, to achieve both implementation extensibility and performance scalability.

Omega's approach reflects a greater focus on scalability, but makes it harder to enforce global properties, such as capacity, fairness, and deadlines.

For more information, refer to `http://research.google.com/pubs/pub41684.html`.

Corona

Corona is another work from **Facebook**, which is now open-sourced and hosted on the GitHub repository at `https://github.com/facebookarchive/hadoop-20/tree/master/src/contrib/corona`.

Facebook, with its huge peta-scale quantity of data, suffered serious performance-related issues with the classic MapReduce framework because of the single JobTracker taking care of thousands of jobs and doing a lot of work alone.

In order to solve these issues, Facebook created Corona, which separated cluster resource management from job coordination.

In Hadoop Corona, the cluster resources are tracked by a central Cluster Manager. Each job gets its own Corona Job Tracker which tracks just that particular job.

Corona has entirely redesigned MapReduce architecture to bring better cluster utilization and job scheduling, just like YARN did.

Facebook's goals in re-writing the Hadoop scheduling framework were not the same as YARN's. Facebook wanted quick improvements in MapReduce, but only the part that they were using. They had no interest in running multiple heterogeneous frameworks such as YARN does or other key design considerations of YARN.

For Facebook, doing a quick rewrite of the scheduler seemed feasible and low risk, compared to going with YARN, getting features that were not needed, understanding it, fixing its problems and then landing up with something that didn't address the primary goal of lowering latency.

The following are some of the key differences:

- Corona does **push-based scheduling** and has an event-driven, callback-oriented message flow. This was critical to achieving fast, low-latency scheduling. Polling is a big part of why the Hadoop scheduler is slow and has scalability issues. YARN does not do callback-based message flow.
- In Corona, JobTracker can run on the same JVM as the Job Client (that is Hive). Facebook had *fat* client machines with tons of RAM and CPU. To reduce latency, maximum processing on the client machine is preferred. In YARN, Job Tracker has to be scheduled within the cluster. This means that there's one extra step between starting a query and getting it running.

- Corona is structured as a contrib project to Hadoop 0.20 branch and is not a very large code base.
- Corona is integrated with the fair-scheduler. YARN is more interested in the capacity scheduler.

For more information on Corona, refer to `https://www.facebook.com/notes/facebook-engineering/under-the-hood-scheduling-mapreduce-jobs-more-efficiently-with-corona/10151142560538920`.

Summary

We talked about various works related to YARN that are available on the market today. These systems share common inspiration/requirements, and the high-level goal of improving scalability, latency, fault-tolerance, and programming-model flexibility. The varied architectural differences are due to the diverse and varied design priorities. In the next chapter, we will talk about YARN's future and support in the industry.

10
YARN – Future and Support

YARN is the new modern data operating system for Hadoop 2. YARN acts as a central orchestrator to support mixed workloads/programming models, running multiple engines, and multiple access patterns such as batch processing, interactive, streaming, and real-time, in Hadoop 2.

In this chapter, we will talk about YARN's journey and its present and future in the big data industry.

What YARN means to the big data industry

It can be said that YARN is a boon to the big data industry. Without YARN the entire big data industry would have been at serious risk. As the industry started playing with big data, new and emerging varieties of problems came into the picture and hence new frameworks.

YARN's support to run these new and emerging frameworks allows these frameworks to focus on solving the problems for which they were specifically meant for, while YARN takes care of resource management and other necessary things (resource allocation, scheduling jobs, fault tolerance, and so on).

Had there been no YARN, these frameworks would have had to do all the resource-management on their own. There are many big data projects that failed in the past due to unrealistic expectations on immature technologies.

YARN is the enabler for porting mature and enterprise-class technologies directly onto Hadoop. Without YARN, the only thing in Hadoop was to use MapReduce.

Journey – present and future

Around two years back, YARN was introduced with the **Hadoop 0.23** release on 11 Nov, 2011.

Since then, there was no looking back and there were a number of releases.

Finally, on October 15, 2013 **Apache Hadoop 2.2.0** was the GA (General Availability) release of Apache Hadoop 2.x.

In October 2013, Apache Hadoop YARN won the **Best Paper award at ACM SoCC (Symposium on Cloud Computing) 2013**.

Apache Hadoop 2.x, powered by YARN, is no doubt the best platform for all of the Hadoop ecosystem components such as MapReduce, Apache Hive, Apache Pig, and so on that use HDFS as the underlying data storage.

YARN was also honored by other open source communities for frameworks such as Apache Giraph, Apache Tez, Apache Spark, Apache Flink, and many others.

Vendors such as **HP**, **Microsoft**, **SAS**, **Teradata**, **SAP**, **Red Hat**, and the list goes on, are moving towards YARN to run their existing products and services on Hadoop.

People willing to modify applications can already use YARN directly, but there are many customers/vendors who don't want to modify their existing application. For them, there is **Apache Slider**, another open source project from Hortonworks, which can deploy any existing distributed applications without requiring them to be ported to YARN.

Apache Slider allows you to bridge existing always-on services and makes sure they work really well on top of YARN, without having to modify the application itself.

Slider facilitates many long-running services and applications such as Apache Storm, Apache HBase, Apache Accumulo, and so on running on YARN.

This initiative will definitely expand the spectrum of applications and use cases that one can actually use with Hadoop and YARN in future.

Present on-going features

Now, let's discuss the present on-going works in YARN.

Long Running Applications on Secure Clusters (YARN-896)

Support long-lived applications and long-lived containers. Refer to `https://issues.apache.org/jira/browse/YARN-896`.

Application Timeline Server (YARN-321, YARN-1530)

Currently, we have a JobHistoryServer for MapReduce history. The MapReduce job history server currently needs to be deployed as a trusted server in sync with the MapReduce runtime. Every new application would need a similar application history server. Having to deploy O (T*V) (where T is the number of type of application, V is the number of version of application) trusted servers is clearly not scalable.

This JIRA is to create only one trusted application history server, which can have a generic UI. Refer to the following links for more information:

- `https://issues.apache.org/jira/browse/YARN-321`
- `https://issues.apache.org/jira/browse/YARN-1530`

Disk scheduling (YARN-2139)

Support for disk as a resource in YARN. YARN should consider disk as another resource for scheduling tasks on nodes, isolation at runtime, and spindle locality. Refer to `https://issues.apache.org/jira/browse/YARN-2139`.

Reservation-based scheduling (YARN-1051)

To extend the YARN RM to handle time explicitly, allowing users to *reserve* capacity over time. This is an important step towards SLAs, long-running services, workflows, and helps in gang scheduling.

Future features

Let's discuss the future works in YARN.

Container Resizing (YARN-1197)

The current YARN resource management logic assumes that the resources allocated to a container are fixed during its lifetime. When users want to change the resources of an allocated container, the only way is releasing it and allocating a new container with the expected size. Allowing runtime changes to the resources of an allocated container will give us better control of resource usage on the application side. Refer to `https://issues.apache.org/jira/browse/YARN-1197`.

Admin labels (YARN-796)

Support for admins to specify labels for nodes. The examples of labels are OS, processor architecture, and so on. Refer to `https://issues.apache.org/jira/browse/YARN-796`.

Container Delegation (YARN-1488)

Allow containers to delegate resources to another container. This would allow external frameworks to share not just YARN's resource-management capabilities, but also its workload-management capabilities.

This also shows that YARN is not only focused on the Apache Hadoop ecosystem components, but also on any existing external non-Hadoop products and services that want to use Hadoop.

Also, work is going on in bringing together the worlds of Data and PaaS by using **Docker**, **Google Kubernetes**, and **Red Hat OpenShift** on YARN so that a common resource management can be done across data and PaaS workloads.

YARN-supported frameworks

The following is the current list of frameworks that runs on top of YARN, and this list will go on getting longer in the future:

- Apache Hadoop MapReduce and its ecosystem components
- Apache HAMA
- OpenMPI
- Apache S4
- Apache Spark
- Apache Tez
- Impala
- Storm
- HOYA (HBase on YARN)
- Apache Samza
- Apache Giraph
- Apache Accumulo
- Apache Flink
- KOYA (Kafka on YARN)
- Solr

Summary

In this chapter, we briefly talked about YARN's journey since its inception. YARN has completely changed Hadoop from the way it was earlier in the Hadoop 1.x version. Now YARN is a first-class resource management framework for supporting mixed workloads/processing frameworks.

From what can been seen and predicted, YARN is surely a hit in the big data industry and has many more new and promising features to come in the future. Currently, YARN handles memory and CPU and will coordinate additional resources such as disk and network I/O in the future.

Index

N

O

P

R

S

T

W

Y

Z

Thank you for buying
YARN Essentials

About Packt Publishing

Packt, pronounced 'packed', published its first book, *Mastering phpMyAdmin for Effective MySQL Management*, in April 2004, and subsequently continued to specialize in publishing highly focused books on specific technologies and solutions.

Our books and publications share the experiences of your fellow IT professionals in adapting and customizing today's systems, applications, and frameworks. Our solution-based books give you the knowledge and power to customize the software and technologies you're using to get the job done. Packt books are more specific and less general than the IT books you have seen in the past. Our unique business model allows us to bring you more focused information, giving you more of what you need to know, and less of what you don't.

Packt is a modern yet unique publishing company that focuses on producing quality, cutting-edge books for communities of developers, administrators, and newbies alike. For more information, please visit our website at `www.packtpub.com`.

About Packt Open Source

In 2010, Packt launched two new brands, Packt Open Source and Packt Enterprise, in order to continue its focus on specialization. This book is part of the Packt Open Source brand, home to books published on software built around open source licenses, and offering information to anybody from advanced developers to budding web designers. The Open Source brand also runs Packt's Open Source Royalty Scheme, by which Packt gives a royalty to each open source project about whose software a book is sold.

Writing for Packt

We welcome all inquiries from people who are interested in authoring. Book proposals should be sent to `author@packtpub.com`. If your book idea is still at an early stage and you would like to discuss it first before writing a formal book proposal, then please contact us; one of our commissioning editors will get in touch with you.

We're not just looking for published authors; if you have strong technical skills but no writing experience, our experienced editors can help you develop a writing career, or simply get some additional reward for your expertise.

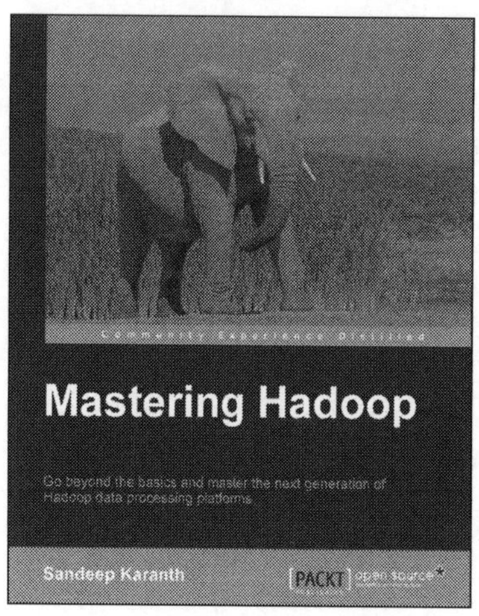

Mastering Hadoop

ISBN: 978-1-78398-364-3 Paperback: 374 pages

Go beyond the basics and master the next generation of Hadoop data processing platforms

1. Learn how to optimize Hadoop MapReduce, Pig and Hive.
2. Dive into YARN and learn how it can integrate Storm with Hadoop.
3. Understand how Hadoop can be deployed on the cloud and gain insights into analytics with Hadoop.

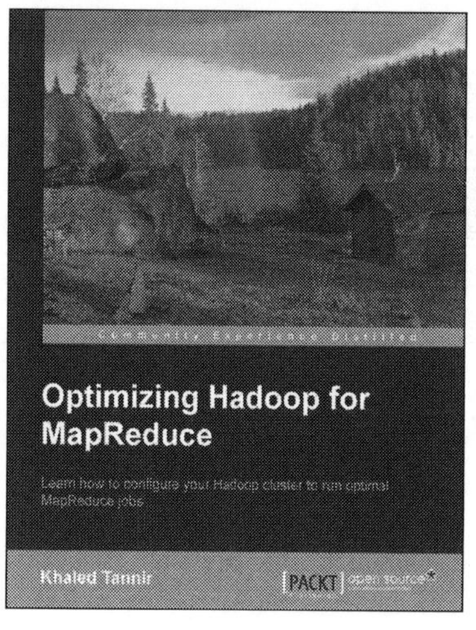

Optimizing Hadoop for MapReduce

ISBN: 978-1-78328-565-5 Paperback: 120 pages

Learn how to configure your Hadoop cluster to run optimal MapReduce jobs

1. Optimize your MapReduce job performance.
2. Identify your Hadoop cluster's weaknesses.
3. Tune your MapReduce configuration.

Please check **www.PacktPub.com** for information on our titles

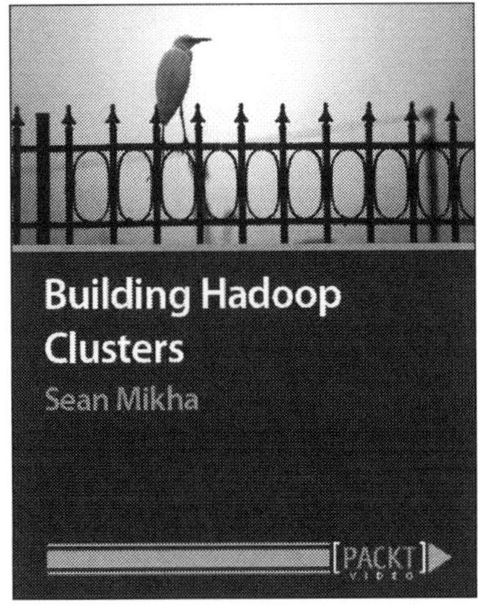

Building Hadoop Clusters [Video]

ISBN: 978-1-78328-403-0 Duration: 02:34 hrs

Deploy multi-node Hadoop clusters to harness the Cloud for storage and large-scale data processing

1. Familiarize yourself with Hadoop and its services, and how to configure them.
2. Deploy compute instances and set up a three-node Hadoop cluster on Amazon.
3. Set up a Linux installation optimized for Hadoop.

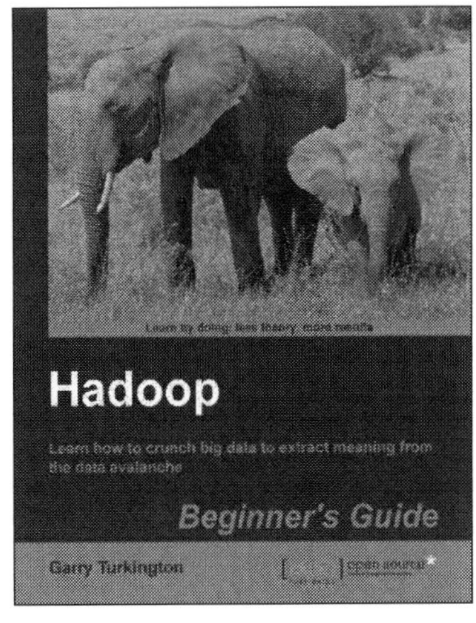

Hadoop Beginner's Guide

ISBN: 978-1-84951-730-0 Paperback: 398 pages

Learn how to crunch big data to extract meaning from the data avalanche

1. Learn tools and techniques that let you approach big data with relish and not fear.
2. Shows how to build a complete infrastructure to handle your needs as your data grows.
3. Hands-on examples in each chapter give the big picture while also giving direct experience.

Made in the USA
San Bernardino, CA
07 April 2015